MIDNIGHT
LIGHTNING

Drawing by Deidra Harris Kelley

MIDNIGHT LIGHTNING

JIMI HENDRIX
AND THE BLACK EXPERIENCE

GREG TATE

Lawrence Hill Books

An imprint of Chicago Review Press, Inc.

Library of Congress Cataloging-in-Publication Data
Tate, Greg.
    Midnight lightning : Jimi Hendrix and the black experience /
    Greg Tate.— 1st ed.
    p. cm.
    ISBN 1-55652-469-2 (cloth)
    1. Hendrix, Jimi. 2. Rock musicians—United States—Biography.
  3. African American musicians—Biography. I. Title.
    ML410.H476T38 2003
787.87′ 166′092—dc21   2003004071

Cover and interior design: Rattray Design

Published by Lawrence Hill Books
An imprint of Chicago Review Press, Incorporated
814 North Franklin Street
Chicago, Illinois 60610
ISBN 1-55652-469-2
Printed in the United States of America
5 4 3 2 1

for these other dark angels,
more recently fallen to earth

June Jordan
Jam Master Jay
Lisa "Left Eye" Lopes
Aaliyah

Jimi was crouched down outside his motel room with several guitars spread out on the tarmac in front of him, a silver conch belt around his hips, white calf-length boots, gypsy waistcoat, a purple shirt, the box of colored inks and oils alongside his guitars.

He was quite alone.

I stood and watched a minute.

It was like the Navajo dream—the warrior before the hunt . . .

This was really the first time Jimi had the chance to play before his own people.

So he just went for it. And he had special guitars he was going to sacrifice for the gig that he'd been saving. The afternoon before he painted them out in the sun.

He looked more and more like a Native American to me as the weekend went on.

He started out as a Black American on Friday night. Saturday night he was a Comanche. By Sunday night he was an Apache warrior, just out to kill.

Eric Burdon, Monterey, 1967

I don't like to be misunderstood by anything or anybody. So if I want to wear a red bandana and turquoise slacks, and if I want my hair down to my ankles, well, that's me. They don't know what's running through my blood. Shit, I'm representing everything as far as I'm concerned.

Jimi Hendrix, 1969

Nobody knew him. "Get off so we can hear Big Maybelle." "Who is this Jimi Hendrix?" "Jimmy who? Jimmy Witherspoon?" He started making some kind of distortion out of his guitar, feeling the public, like throwing something at them. And the audience replied with an egg, someone threw an egg out the window and it really freaked him out. He started playing like he'd never played before. . . . That was his first communication with Black people and they dug him.

Arthur Allen, Harlem, 1969

CONTENTS

ACKNOWLEDGMENTS

Tundera and Taharqa Aleem for boundless generosity of time, memories, and spirit; Craig Street and Ronny Drayton for years of brotherly love; Xenobia Bailey for being a griot; Michaela Angela Davis, Aunjanue Ellis, Lisa Jones, Raquel Cepeda, Kandia Crazy Horse, dream hampton, and Doreen Bowens for the sisterly lovetaps; Burnt Sugar, especially Kirk Douglas, Rene Akhan, and Lisala Beatty, for keeping the Hendrix flame stoked in our band; Yuval Taylor for being as long-suffering and on-point an editor as a writer could ever want; Jim Rutman for the back-court motion; Diedra Harris-Kelley for her dark and lovely graphite work; photographer Laurie Lyons and *Untold* magazine for the author's chunky air guitar moment; Butch Morris, Vernon Reid, Melvin Gibbs, Graham Haynes for the inside scoop; Stephanie Kelly for the donation of her third eye to the proceedings; Krista Franklin for the poems; and for being from Dayton, Ohio, like the author, Jared Nickerson, and Paul Laurence Dunbar.

MIDNIGHT LIGHTNING

MEDITATIONS

All roads lead to Jimi Hendrix.

As all roads veer off from Hendrix, guiding us toward whatever promised land, crossroads, or dystopia we may choose to imagine. It is as if all of human history and mythology had conspired to deposit him on our doorsteps.

This living embodiment of all our racial fears, romantic fancies, otherworldly dreams, and radical desires. This shy Black man bursting with reflections of all the culture's fecundity and fetishes—what rough beast set his godhead before us and instructed him to roam about so unchained and uncaged, so unbowed and unbound? A beast kind enough, at the end of the day, to let us catch him going about his business of peace, noise, unity, and levitation.

So that if the question was ever "Mr. Hendrix, are you now or have you ever been Buddhist or Baptist, Republican or Democrat, Panther or peacenik, hawk or dove, cowboy or

Indian, Jew or Gentile, Black or hippie?," his answer could only be "Undeclared, but yes, all of the above, *in my experience*."

This is why, even now, so long after his bloody, bile-filled end, his corpus (that essential body of works) still resounds throughout so many lands and remains seductive to so many among our species, overcoming geography, faith, and ethnicity in a single bound.

Hendrixian: what we ought to mean whenever we speak of the universal. *Hendrixian:* what we ought to mean whenever we recognize this as A Black Planet. Because it is through him that we finally see what connects our griots and their koras to our Greeks and their lyres, and our cantors and our Jolsons to our Buffalo Soldiers and their banjos, and our slow sliding blues troubadours to all the other fallen Orphic angels who exchanged their wings for the garden of earthly delights—Shango, Apollo, Thor, the whole lot of them, aye, Mr. Delany and Lucifer too.

It was to be through him that some came to finally believe in gods on earth—like my African American postman friend who, one night outside of Frank's Lounge in Brooklyn, insisted that if I was writing about Hendrix I had to say that "he really was a God and not just a guitar player."

Long after his expulsion from the garden, his nervous system covers the earth. Like those maps of aerial flight paths they hand out on transatlantic jumbos. Like those spindly-creepy networks of arterial foliage you used to find in the *Encylopaedia Britannica*'s translucent anatomical overlays.

And the *Britannica* is where we must go should we desire to summon all his common ancestors. Because it's hard to imagine there having ever been a Hendrix without there having first been the Dionysus of *The Bacchae* or the Debussy of *Le Mer* or the Varèse of *Poème Electronique* or the Elvis Presley of Sun

Studios (the same Presley who turned out a sixteen-year-old Hendrix in 1957 at Seattle's Sicks Stadium where he saw The King melt down a crowd of 15,000). We say had there been no Robert Johnson, no Arthur Rimbaud, no *A Love Supreme*, or no Lord Buckley there may have been no Jimi Hendrix either. We say, Lookahere, man, Captain Blood and Sitting Bull bear as much responsibility for him coming this way as Orpheus, Orson Welles, and Philip José Farmer (the same Farmer of science fiction fame whose short story about aliens from a planet with a purple hazy atmosphere, not an acid trip like we once thought, inspired the song). Go tell the world: Ogun, Lawrence of Arabia, Jocko Henderson, and Iceberg Slim aren't the only ones who have to take the weight. Don't just turn the evil eye on John Lee Hooker, Willie Dixon, and Ike Turner. Train your gaze on Jean Genet, Johann Sebastian Bach, Sun Ra, and Karlheinz Stockhausen too. Don't just blame old blind Homer, Uncle Remus, the Bronze Buckaroo, and Blind Lemon Jefferson: Ravi Shankar and John Glenn got some owning up to do as well. Let none of them off the hook: not Little Richard (whose Cadillac once presciently and innocently pulled up in front of Hendrix's house in Seattle seven years before Jimi would join his band) nor the Bard of Avon, Lady Day, Bird, Josephine Baker, or the Mensa genius Jayne Mansfield (whom Hendrix recorded a 45 with). Paternity tests for Chuck Yeager, the Isley Brothers, and Oscar Wilde will all come out positive. So that when the court (Judge Pigmeat Markham presiding) says, "Jimi Hendrix, the bench finds you guilty of descent from a long line of barnstormers, runaway slaves, carnival freaks, and social deviants—Nigga, how do you plead?," his defense, wrought of iron, catgut, and Spanish fly, will be the Fender Strat–Marshall stack version of "Strong and Wrong, Loud and Proud, Black and Blue, Who the Hell Asked You?"

As his own mad children can't ever stop themselves from cussing up a storm or brazenly exhibiting the stigmata and stain of his mark. Roll call: David Bowie, Evel Knievel, Bootsy Collins, and DJ Shadow. Chris Whitley and KISS. David Murray, James Newton, and Butch Morris. Neil Gaiman, Todd McFarlane, and Ishmael Reed. William Gibson, Lucas Samaras, and DJ Spooky. Betty Davis, Zaha Hadid, and the Bomb Squad. Jeff Mills, Alice Walker, and Ikue Mori. The Pharcyde, Susie Ibarra, and Me'Shell NdegéOcello. Roll call: Patti Smith, Jean-Michel Basquiat, Tracey Emin, AR Kane, Simon Reynolds's Generation Ecstasy, and Colson Whitehead.

A god can do it. But will you tell me how
a man can enter through the lyre's strings?
Our mind is split. And at the shadowed crossing
of heart-roads, there is no temple for Apollo.

Song, as you have taught it, is not desire,
not wooing any grace that can be achieved;
song is reality. Simple, for a god.
But when can we be real? When does he pour

the earth, the stars, into us? Young man,
it is not your loving, even if your mouth
was forced wide open by your voice—learn

to forget that passionate music. It will end.
True singing is a different breath, about
nothing. A gust inside the god. A wind.

Rainer Maria Rilke, *Sonnets to Orpheus* I: 3
(translated by Stephen Mitchell)

A mess of ungodly desires will follow his time on this bitter earth.

His here-todays and hereafter-tomorrows will come to have dire, mortal consequences for many of diminished capacity. Because of him the notion of human limits will become far too ludicrous for words. Because of him that timeworn axiom of the sensual adventurer, "the kingdom of excess leads to the palace of wisdom," will suddenly seem quaint. Astral traveling will become a plebeian affair. A trip no further out of reach to the hoi polloi than the nearest stylus. Yes, Lord, yes, a lot of bad music, ill-advised drug consumption, and garish costuming will result from his influence. Shitloads of gnat-note fusion jazz and overwrought instrumental metal too. But these homages and mindless, adolescent diversions will neither mean nor cause any great harm. For all were just feeble attempts to march in lock-step with the Almighty.

(It is not easy to write about Hendrix without indulging in hagiography, hyperbole, superlatives. We have no interest in even trying. Because what a bore that would be.)

I: 7

Praising is what matters! He was summoned for that,
and came to us like the ore from a stone's
Silence. His mortal heart presses out
a deathless, inexhaustible wine.

Whenever he feels the god's paradigm grip
his throat, the voice does not die in his mouth.
All becomes vineyard, all becomes grape,
ripened on the hills of his sensuous South.

Neither decay in the sepulchre of kings
nor any shadow that has fallen from the gods
can ever detract from his glorious praising.

For he is a herald who is with us always,
holding far into the doors of the dead
a bowl with ripe fruit worthy of praise.

(TALKIN' ABOUT) MY
RACIAL AGENDA

However:

Like Tricky Dick, let's make one thing perfectly clear. Let us be crystal clear, as our fallen comrade Kwame Ture né Stokely Carmichael used to insist. Let us also make it plain, as our dearly departed brother Malcolm X demanded of all who rock the mic. Let no one bitch and moan later over how they were tricked, misled, lied to, hoodwinked, or bamboozled. If the booming racial markers above are not warning enough let's just say, This is not Everyman's Guide to Jimi Hendrix. No, this is a Jimi Hendrix book with A Racial Agenda. A Jimi book with plantation baggage, darkskin biases, and Black Power axes to grind. Even more pompously, it purports to be a book of ideas about Hendrix. A book bent on making philosophical judgment calls regarding his race, his romance, his tools. Race, sex, technology, and Jimi Hendrix—these will position the coordinates on this star map.

We want to be duly recorded as more obsessed about the Blackness of Hendrix than about his life experiences or music per se, though these are unavoidable signposts unless your name is Lacan, Barthes, Derrida, Kristeva, or Baudrillard—and honey, we ain't even.

This man Hendrix continues to jack up all of our hidebound notions about how the world's supposed to function—racially, sexually, technologically—and for this mucking about he deserves his own *Mythologies* or *Grammatology*, and one day, by Jove, he will have them. But this modest endeavor which must speak about the social meaning of Jimi Hendrix and the sexual mystery of Jimi Hendrix and the scientific inquiries of Jimi Hendrix also proposes to be something even cruder than that: a Jimi Hendrix Primer for Blackfolk. A user-friendly introduction for all of My People who don't get that Hendrix was a Black man who came from several Black worlds to make extraterrestrial Black music for all God's children whether they got rhythm or not.

This Jimi Hendrix book then will try to be many things to many people, probably pleasing few in the process, but know ye this: foremost it is intended to function as a Jimi Hendrix Reclamation Project. One that dares come demanding he be accepted in the fold of twentieth-century Black icons by all who ever dared think he played "whiteboy music."

Now to all you ecumenical types, we say, Never fear. To all who've embraced Hendrix as their color-blind savior, we say, Never fear. We will accomplish our mission without denying Hendrix, Universal Redneck Solvent and Racial Paradigm Shifter, his due. Indeed we swear on a stack of uncracked Gideon Bibles, no short shrift shall be given his transformative impact on music lovers of all phenotypes and color schemes.

Just know that we won't be skating over King James Marshall Hendrix's (not just) knee-deep roots in the African American jungle boogie either.

Since Race in America is not a simple subject, there's no reason to expect Race and Jimi Hendrix will be either. Like theologians awestruck before the mysteries of a sacred text or historians befuddled by the course and meaning of an age, we stand before the topic of Hendrix and race expecting Confusion, Bewilderment, and Paradox to be our three-headed dog at the gate, our Gnostic gospels of the day.

This is not another Hendrix biography, memoir, or companion per se, though it shamelessly draws upon the work of others who have done that sort of work exceedingly well: David Henderson, Charles Schaar Murray, Johnny Black, Kathy Etchingham, John McDermott, Eddie Kramer, Harry Shapiro, and Caesar Glebeek to name but a few notables from the Hendrix bibliotheca. We've just got other fish to fry.

For better or worse, this is a book of strange ideas about a long-dead still enigmatic major dude whose contributions to the American race comedy only appear curiouser and curiouser as time goes on. Some of these strange ideas sprang from my head alone: I made them up, I'll claim them as such, and I have no problem letting the chips fall where they may. Other of these notions derive (and keep arriving) from friends and fellow travelers—a few of whom actually knew Hendrix back in the day and even before that day. Classical anthropology types would classify them as informants, but they're just my buds, y'all: a handpicked cadre of opinionated negroes who have their own pointed thoughts and opinions about the man, his mysteries, and their chthonic meanings. I speak now about Xenobia Bailey, Ronnie Drayton, Craig Street, Michaela Angela Davis, and The Twins. (The Twins are the best known of this bunch among Hendrix cognôscenti, but hardly well known enough as

Hendrix griots. Having sung on the posthumous releases *Cry of Love*, *War Heroes*, and *Rainbow Bridge* as the Ghetto Fighters, The Twins are also the Artists Formerly Known as the Aleems. Born Arthur and Albert Allen, they recorded under that name in the 1980s. They now go by the names Tundera and Taharqa Aleem and reside comfortably in the Bedford Stuyvesant section of Brooklyn. These days you'll find them working as nutritionists, weight trainers, and mind enhancers with hiphop MCs such as MC Lyte, Busta Rhymes, and Noriega. Theirs has been a long strange trip that will here be given ample room to properly unfold and be properly told.)

Recognizing Hendrix as a major African American artist with thorny and extensive branches reaching all over-under-across what we leftover '70s types tag The Black Experience can get ugly. Going there has proven to be an indelicate task at best. Expect trunkloads of feather boas to be ruffled while small armies of Afro-picks, Huey Newton posters, and blue suede shoes get moshed on in the process.

3

RACE, RAMA, AND THE GREAT AFRICAN AMERICAN ROLL CALL

Any book about Hendrix with race on the brain has no choice but to recognize him as a destroyer of our racialist worldviews. This holds for Black and white folk alike.

Let's face it: in one fell swoop he forever swept aside the misapprehension that rock stars could only be young white and British and that said experimental Black pop musicians ought to look no further than the chitlin circuit or jazz lofts for resources. A profound irony of Hendrix's career is that even after shredding racial shibboleths by the dozens he discovered a gate at the country's color-obsessed edge he was not able to bust wide. This being the same gate that has kept Black people from embracing him as one of their own to this day. The one that reads, "Jimi Hendrix was different from you and me: Jimi Hendrix was for white people."

All boundary crossers face the inherent problem of coming back. In Hendrix's case, his timing could not have been worse. Here after all was a Black artist who stepped way on the other side of America's racial/musical/political divide at a time when lines were being drawn in the sand—when Blackfolk were being hustled, harangued, and harassed into choosing sides and signing race-war blood oaths. Who was this Jimi Hendrix who had the nerve, the unmitigated gall, to be glaringly beloved by The Devilish White Man when many Black spokespersons, self-anointed or otherwise, were questioning what there was to love about anything white? (Though even at this pitched moment the marvel of human complexity remained intact. Just ask my man Lewis "Flip" Barnes who tells the story of how it was his rabidly anti-white Black Panther cousin Stevie who practically forced him to see Hendrix perform live when Flip thought Jimi was "nothing but a hippie Uncle Tom.")

Identifying Hendrix as A Black Man and A Black Icon is not a particularly courageous task this late in the post–Black Power day, but it will still strike some as wrongheaded and perverse. Look in your conventional Black Hall of Heroes and you will not see Hendrix leaping out from the dioramas. Now just between us postmodernists, we all know hero worship is supposed to be passé, dead, like "The Author" or "The Great Men of History." Except I sometimes also live over on this other world called the post-Soul world, where the credo Black Is Mo' Beautiful lives on, even if in more commodified form today than in the '60s. In this other world, that of the lapsed Cultural Nationalist turned Pro-Black Consumer, the Hero continues to battle the forces of white supremacy in order to regain his throne as Earth's Rightful Ruler. In this world there's a pantheon and a time line of Major Black Figures: those called upon and chosen to uplift The Culture. We speak now of people who did The Work That Had to Be Done, singular and courageous figures who took up the task of repairing and carrying the fractured, fragmented fightback folly that is The Black Psyche around on their shoulders like a kleig light.

My own Time of the Heroes begins somewhere around the advent of our great emancipators and abolitionists—Frederick Douglass, Harriet Tubman, and Sojourner Truth. It continues unabated with our great educators, world shakers, and institution builders of the early twentieth century—Booker T. Washington, W. E. B. Du Bois, Ida B. Wells, Marcus Garvey, Mary McCleod Bethune, Madame C. J. Walker. Come the Jazz Age and the real Godfathers and Godmothers of Soul step up to the plate: Langston Hughes, Zora Neale Hurston, Louis Armstrong, Duke Ellington, Count Basie, and A. Phillip Randolph. The superheroic terms Race Man and Race Woman come into being somewhere around this time. A stampede of X-Men types rapidly emerge to Africanize European epistemological systems. Roll call: Thelonious Monk, Charlie Parker, Dizzy Gillespie, Max Roach, Billie Holiday, Miles Davis, Charles Mingus, Randy Weston, Yusef Lateef, John Coltrane, Ornette Coleman, Lorraine Hansberry, Nat King Cole.

By the 1960s we're on some Julius Lester Look out whitey Black Power's Gonna Get Your Mama type shit: Roll call: Aretha Franklin, Martin Luther King, Malcolm X, Rosa Parks, Fannie Lou Hamer, Bob Moses, Berry Gordy, Sam Cooke, Otis Redding, Chuck Berry, Little Richard, Muddy Waters, Howlin' Wolf, Richard Wright, James Baldwin, Romare Bearden, Roy De Carava, Elizabeth Catlett, James Brown, the Temptations, Sugar Ray Robinson, Muhammad Ali, Sidney Poitier, Bill Russell, Sly Stone, Huey Newton, Stevie Wonder, Marvin Gaye, Hal Bennett, Toni Morrison, Leon Forrest, Ernest Gaines, Charlene Hatcher-Polite. By the 1970s and 1980s thinking Black has become synonymous with thinking for yourself and with mainstream success. Roll call: Toni Morrison, Ntozake Shange, Alice Walker,

Richard Pryor, George Clinton, Prince, Michael Jackson, Bob Marley, Charles Burnett, Bad Brains, Grandmaster Flash and the Furious Five, Minister Louis Farrakhan, Russell Simmons, Julie Dash, Public Enemy, Biggie Smalls, Tupac Shakur, RZA, Chris Rock, Denzel Washington. (And after all of that, recognize Jimi Hendrix as the forerunner of run-amok Black Individualism understood as the supreme form of Black Consciousness/Black Entrepreneurship.)

In the throne room of the Black and Iconic in the twentieth century all these other figures have been given grand featured roles. The thing with Hendrix is some simpleminded folk can't accept that Hendrix was as much their brother as he was brother (and deity) to his fellow guitar-rocking stars Keith Richards, Jimmy Page, Pete Townsend, Jeff Beck, George Harrison, John McLaughlin, and Duane Allman—all of whom just happened to be white.

As intimated earlier, Hendrix came along at a time in world history when only white boys were supposed to be handed rock star badges and the loudest, angriest Blackfolk around were bent on getting whitey off the planet. What a revolting predicament, as my man Ben Grimm would say. But he made it work for him. (There is after all an argument to be made for Hendrix having invented the rock star as we know it—the irrepressible flaunting of wealth, glamour, gear, and girls. Certainly he was the man for whom the term Guitar God was invented, all that "Clapton is God" graffiti from apocryphal London toilet stalls notwithstanding.) Well, except with Black people, and here's why: see, Hendrix wasn't just a racial-political heretic but a musical one as well. And I believe, even if no one else does, that a fair part of Blackfolk's disavowal of any knowledge of Hendrix's actions comes from the fact that he made the guitar matter more to the world than The Voice of God, or at least its living, breathing manifestation, The Soul Singer. (This assessment of The Soul Singer as The Voice of God comes from my photographer/raconteur pal Jules Allen, who holds the faith that all the great male soul singers were destined to become tragedies—Sam Cooke, Frankie Lymon, Jackie Wilson, Little Willie John, James Brown, Otis Redding, David Ruffin, Teddy Pendergrass, James Carr, Al "Grits" Green, Curtis Mayfield, Bob Marley, the whole lot of them—because they were walking around with the prophetic voice of god, doing all manner of ungodly things with it, and so came by their martyrdom super-naturally.)

In the Jesus- and Sam Cooke–loving Black world of '50s and '60s rhythm and blues, guitarists were sidebars, those sometimes entertaining fellows kept barely audible to the Amen Corner and the panty-tossing gals in the front rows. A distant second fiddle, if that, to singers, sword swallowers, circus clowns, talking dog acts, wooden dummies, and barbaric bar-walking tenor men like Big Jay McNeely and the Lynn Hope character immortalized in Amiri Baraka's tale "The Screamers." Even in jazz, guitars rarely got to duke it out with the more stalwart and loudspoken trumpets, trombones, and tenor saxophones—not even in the anarchic days of free jazz. "Turn that damn guitar down" remains a hallmark of guitarist, vocalist, and horn player interaction in Black music to this day. (This state of affairs might have gone another way if Wes Montgomery had taken Coltrane's offer to join his Village Vanguard band featuring Eric Dolphy or if George Benson had opted to accept Miles Davis's offer to make his '60s group a sextet. In both instances, however, mercantile manager-types convinced their six-string charges to pass in pursuit of greener pastures.)

Hendrix, a man routinely kicked out of rhythm and blues bands for being too loud (in theatrics, dress, and sound), became the guitar's revenge on jazz and rhythm and blues. A punishment fit for trying to push the almighty axe into the wings if not the organ-trio dustbin of musical history. This is why nearly three decades after Hendrix's demise the apex of animal magnetism and fuckability in American pop is a skinny (white) guy with a screaming guitar, not a pimped-out Voice of God on his knees yelping, Please, baby please, baby, baby, baby, please. The soul man's plea for love remains long and strong on the Black side of the tracks, but even there the perception that white rockboys are sex gods while soulmen are merely well-sung, well-hung (but sensitive) primitives holds arguably fast.

The ironic disjunction between Hendrix's superstar status among whites and his Whodat? status in Black America begs a few questions: Just how Black was Jimi Hendrix's music, really? How sexy was he to Black women, then and now? And how soulful and inventive was his art by jazz and rhythm and blues standards as well? Thirty-something years after his departure from this plane of existence you'd think Hendrix's virtuosity and whip-appeal couldn't be hotly contested questions, but they are, if only by dint of how uncanonized he remains among African Americans as compared to whitefolk. (Yes, we're going *there* too.)

As is the case with most Black geniuses, Hendrix defied and damn near snapped the measuring stick of Black and white America's cultural authenticators. In the wake of feminism, poststructuralism, postmodernity, postcolonial studies, writers on Hendrix have more exegetic tools than before to carefully read his effect on the epistemological landscape. Deconstruction is demanded because, like Jean-Michel Basquiat's (his successor on the nation's racial, sexual, and artistic playing fields), Hendrix's legitimacy as an artist and as a Black man remain in question. The common fate, as it were, of all negroes who draw outside of the lines in Europe-worshipping white America and faux-tribal-homogeneity-worshipping Black America.

4

PLAYING THE RACE GAME

Unlike Miles Davis, who over time seemed to demand racialization, demand his every utterance and gesture be read through a glass darkly (Miles recalled his time at Juilliard as one consumed by the stench of white people; he once expressed that he'd like to spend his last few minutes on earth choking a white man to death), Hendrix was not, by recorded evidence, much of what we in the African American community would classify as a "race-man," a My People First kind of guy, as it were. With much the same modesty he adopted when portraying the sort of gentleman who never bragged about his bedroom exploits (his defenses of his roadtime sexual appetites tend to be coy and feinting, saying everything and nothing in the same breath), Hendrix, as already noted, eschewed focus on his race and racism in conversation.

His mid-career desire to connect with Black audiences probably did make him guilt-trippingly available to entreaties, rough-house and otherwise, from militants. In *A Film About Jimi Hendrix*, The Twins tell a funny story about Hendrix buying a Black Panther paper from a card-carrying brother who tried to embarrass them into copping one too. By his insinuation, if Jimi Hendrix bought a paper surely such real Black men as The Twins would have to. Their unexpected response was curt: "Jimi Hendrix bought a paper because he wanted a paper. We don't." The Twins go on to say Hendrix was taken aback too since he was trying to impress them with how down he could be with Ultra Blackness.

There's no way, though, that Hendrix was naive about how the race game was played in the world. Life in segregated Seattle in the '40s and '50s and in Kentucky where he was stationed while an Army man in the '60s surely left plenty of scars under the skin. The chitlin circuit's separate and unequal constellation of ghetto bars, roadside joints, swank theatres, and fancy-dan nightclubs, those places where Black artists had no choice but to make their stand (as Hendrix paid his dues with Wilson Pickett, Gorgeous George, Little Richard, the Isley Brothers, King Curtis, and Ike Turner) would have quickly seen to that.

But Hendrix had sky-high musical ambitions, not least being to play a kind of high-volume phantasmagorical guitar music that required white patronage and demanded he not be read as racially threatening or intimidating. He was also from that side of African American consciousness, per Ralph Ellison, which sees racist refusals not as obstacles but as strategic opportunities.

(It is, ironically, because Hendrix's race attracted so little attention from his white supporters that his racial affinities draw so many questions today. The sort of pronounced absence-in-presence so profound it can't not incite a little blowback; e.g., "What do you mean you never thought of Hendrix as Black? What is it Black people are supposed to be like?" and so forth.)

There are, again, many striking racial anomalies in the Hendrix story—that he had white sidemen backing him up, that he became a success in America without being a rhythm and blues or jazz success story first, and actually, never. The Twins talk about how in the late '60s, at the height of Hendrix's fame, he could travel to Harlem and walk about as unhindered and unrecognized as he did when he was an unknown starving artist. Irony of ironies: in London and the East Village, Hendrix was The Man. In Harlem, he was The Invisible Man. What role did the exclusive, whites-only marketing plan of his management and record label play in this conundrum? How much of Blackfolk's disinterest was because his music held little appeal for people whose tastes ran exclusively to Motown, Southern soul, urban blues, and funky jazz—anything but psychedelic rock? Rhetorical questions to be sure, but telling ones about Hendrix's amazing ability to concoct a music from those same roots that might as well have been of a frequency inaudible to negroes.

James Baldwin once said that to be Black and conscious in America is to be in a constant state of rage, but apparently this axiom did not apply to Jimi. The princely mannered and charming Hendrix was read as "somebody you could take home to your mother," says Mitch Mitchell. He worked his way into white people's hearts without bringing any hint of danger or racial discord or disgust with him. He also was a generational peer of his fellow upstarts in the London rock community. He loved Bob Dylan, read science fiction incessantly, and was frequently heard playing a form of Black music way left of Motown, free jazz, and even Chicago blues, in form and content.

He did have his Blackheart moments though, firing a once-beloved road manager named only H because he crossed the line of Black boss/white employee decorum one innocent morning when he told a bleary-eyed Hendrix he looked like "a gorilla who just had his bananas." Former Soft Machine vocalist Robert Wyatt told Charles Schaar Murray of a Southern tour where an otherwise affable promoter called an exasperating Black waitress a nigger in Hendrix's presence before realizing Hendrix was there and might be offended, which Hendrix quite vociferously was. Murray also recounts the time Hendrix refused to do an interview with an English journalist named Carolyn Coon because he thought her name was a racist joke. On the other hand, the one and only time Hendrix performed in Harlem on a flatbed truck a Black Nationalist brother came up and told him, Brother, it's time for you to come home. To which Hendrix replied, "You got to do what you have to do and I have to do what I have to do. Now!" Hendrix also expressed ambivalent feelings about the Panthers and about the spate of riots that was sweeping the ghettoes—his song "House Burning Down" from *Electric Ladyland* emphatically questions brothers burning their brothers' homes down at a time when Black Panther spokesman H. Rap Brown was serving the molotov doctrine of "Burn baby, burn." He contradicted himself often regarding the Panthers though, sometimes damning with faint praise, other times serving up a more conciliatory sense of their merit: "Get your Black Panthers . . . not to kill anybody but to scare them. I know it sounds like war but that's what's gonna have to happen, it has to be war if nobody is going to do it peacefully. . . . Like quite naturally you say make love not war and all these other things but then you come back to reality and there are some evil folks around and they want you to be passive and weak and peaceful so they can just overtake you like jelly on bread. . . . You have to fight fire with fire."

These sentiments are not so out of line with supposed peacenik Hendrix's comment to an English writer in 1967 about America in Vietnam that sounds as if it came from some right-wing jingoist of the day: "Did you send the Americans away when they landed in Normandy? That was also purely interference. No, but that was concerning your skin. The Americans are fighting in Vietnam for the complete free world. As soon as they move out, they'll be at the mercy of the communists. For that matter, the yellow danger [China] should not be underestimated. Of course war is terrible but at the present it's still the only guarantee to maintain peace."

By the time he began performing his tormented anti-war blues "Machine Gun" (with its cool and coy dedication to "all the soldiers fighting in Chicago and Milwaukee and New York" and then, almost as afterthought, "and oh yes all the soldiers fighting in Vietnam") on New Year's Eve, 1969, Hendrix seems to have rethought allegiance to the American flag in Southeast Asia and the protest movement thereof.

Hendrix was clearly on a journey so far ahead of its time he was out there alone, providing his own means of political, ethical, and artistic direction and validation. No other Black artist was performing the song "Sgt Pepper's Lonely Hearts Club Band" right in front of Paul McCartney and John Lennon two days after the *Sgt Pepper* album had hit the street. No other African American artist of the era would find himself as alienated from the uprising Black community in his home country either.

Writer Lisa Jones's comment (below) about Hendrix possessing a confident but mellow speaking voice also bears further rumination when we recall that most Black men who had mic control in the '60s weren't exactly shrinking violets, wallflowers, shyguys, or Silent Sams. When we recall the Black male voices who had the world's attention back then we hear them shouting things. A lot of coarse sloganeering comes to mind: "Black Power," "Burn, baby, burn," "Power to the people," "Death to the pigs," and whatnot. About Hendrix we always hear "soft-spoken," "demure," "coquettish," "purring." The words people used to characterize Hendrix's speaking voice tend to be 180 degrees away from the riot-act sound of such inflammatory protest rhetoricians as Carmichael, Cleaver, Baraka, and Rap Brown. Hendrix let his guitar do the crying, screaming, and shouting and it ended up getting him as much publicity ink as any rabble rouser of the day. As still occurs today, there is the expectation that when an intelligent Black person gets white folks' attention he has an obligation to speak on behalf of his people. Hendrix's rise and political evolution dovetail with the major transitions that occurred in American race politics between 1965 and 1969. His response to those events, though, would be, customarily, quite distinctly his own.

INVISIBILITY BLUES

There was a lot of fire coming down from the trees but we were all right as long as we kept down. And I was thinking, Oh man, so this is a rice paddy, yes wow! when I suddenly heard an electric guitar shooting right up in my ear and a rapturous Black voice singing, coaxing, "Now c'mon baby, stop acting so crazy." And when I got it all together I turned to see a grinning Black corporal hunched over a cassette recorder. That's the story of the first time I ever heard Jimi Hendrix, but in a war where a lot of people talked about Aretha's "Satisfaction" the way other people speak of Brahms's 4th it was more than a story, it was credentials.... Hendrix had once been in the 101st Airborne and the Airborne in Nam was full of wiggy, brilliant spades like him, really mean and really good guys who took care of you when things got bad. That music meant a lot to them. I never once heard it played over the Armed Forces Radio Network.

Michael Herr, *Dispatches*

Race in America, even in the 21st century, remains a complicated, messy, intricate, and downright tricky affair. In the 1960s it came with unspoken laws, inhibitions, and understandings that make the viperous court manners depicted in *Dangerous Liaisons* read like high school by comparison. When it comes to how an African American man was supposed to act and interact with whites, especially awestruck mongrel hordes of them, Hendrix not only disobeyed the rules, firmly established since the days of Thomas Jefferson, he functioned as if they didn't even exist. In the canon of historical Black icons, Hendrix is somewhat without precedent for being lionized by whites before the Black community even knew or cared he existed.

He was not the first Black American artist to have a substantial, or even predominantly, white consumer base—Scott Joplin, Bessie Smith, Billie Holiday, Paul Robeson, Miles Davis, Nat King Cole, Sammy Davis, Jr., all preceded him. Ben Harper, Tracy Chapman, and Lenny Kravitz may outrace him with regard to the paucity of Black faces at their shows. Conversely, Sly Stone, Hendrix's former employers the Isley Brothers, George Clinton, and hiphop as a genre have all accomplished what Hendrix couldn't: selling hip Black rock to whites and the 'hood without making Blackfolk stare down their noses at they asses like they were alienated Oreos.

Hendrix, however, became an international pop music phenomenon without ever having been even a minor sensation among those useful abstractions, The Black Masses and The Black Community. The reason for this turnabout speaks volumes about the complicated way race politics and race manners can play out in the real world. A world where gatekeepers are made to be trampled underfoot and sent sliding down history's slippery slope by the likes of a Jimi Hendrix.

In America, pop music continues to be racially slotted, targeted, and marketed thirty-five years after Hendrix and the '60s

British rock scene that embraced him underscored Martin Luther King, Jr.'s dreams of a color-blind world. This very fact reflects how segregated this country's culture chooses to remain. Yet Hendrix was both the victim and a beneficiary of the way race circumscribed a Black artist's sense of possibility in 1960s' USA. The very idea that Hendrix left the States with the intention of conquering London's pop world in 1966 seems perfectly logical only in retrospect. (Reportedly, it even seemed at first to Hendrix to be an absolutely foolhardy, quixotic, and unthinkable course of action.) A host of African American artists had of course exiled themselves to Europe before Hendrix—notables such as Josephine Baker, Richard Wright, Kenny Clarke, and Dexter Gordon readily come to mind—but Hendrix didn't leave the States as they did in protest of racism or in pursuit of basic human dignity. Hendrix actually resisted taking the Transatlantic plunge, though he was desperate, tattered, and starving, when new manager Chas Chandler offered him a ticket on the first thing smoking. What is said to have finally won him over was a promise of meeting Eric Clapton, whose wicked stanknasty guitar playing with John Mayall, the Yardbirds, and Cream Hendrix was well aware of. For the wild, young, and competitive James, besting Clapton in musical combat and dethroning him in his own native land became an irresistible clincher in agreeing to answer London's call. (That eventual match-up actually proved something of a walk in the park for Hendrix, as Clapton himself recounts it: "He was very, very flash, even in the dressing room. He stood in front of the mirror and asked if he could play a couple of numbers. He did 'Killing Floor,' a Howling Wolf number I've always wanted to play but which I've never really had the technique to do. It was just, well, he just stole the show.")

By the time Hendrix arrived in England in mid-1966, the Beatles, the Rolling Stones, the Who, Eric Clapton, the

Yardbirds, and the Kinks had not only mounted the so-called British Invasion of the American pop charts, with a sound derived largely from music of African American origin, they had also established the Rock Star as a scandalous and Dionysian second order of royalty and debauchery in British society. (A mounting of the slippery, class-obsessed British social ladder, completed, we may assume, with the recent knighting of Sir Mick Jagger.) The British Rock Stars were not only selling original songs but original sin. Sexuality and sexual androgyny were markers of their movement, and in this aspect Hendrix was to the manner born.

He had in fact come to the attention of Chandler after first gripping the attention of the lovely and literate Linda Keith, then a model and current flame of the Stones' Keith Richards. In his first days and weeks in England, Chandler not only arranged for Hendrix to bowl over the cream of British musicians, like Clapton and the Beatles, but to be given equal opportunity to impress their girlfriends, grandmothers, and groupies.

The body type of the English rock star—narrow-hipped, slim-waisted, slightly emaciated limbs, pouting, girlish features— weren't so unlike Hendrix's wider own, thereby making him an easily objectified, readymade Black version of what they were used to.

This was also a time of a fashion revolution in London, and here too Hendrix arrived as a man more than ready for the haute couture demands of the party. Before we even get to his sound innovations, Hendrix must be understood as a fashion pioneer among his generation of African American men. Largely functioning as his own stylist, he came to define the parameters of rock star haberdashery.

Urban fashion specialist Michaela Angela Davis points out that all of Hendrix's fashion choices were inspired by the warrior esthetic of his various adopted tribes—the long military coats of the British Army; the buckskin fringe, moccasins, and turquoise of his Native American ancestors; the headbands and handkerchiefs of the Gypsy; the kimonos of the Samurai; the velour hats, silk shirts, and conks of the Pimp. On this scene, Hendrix proved to be an extraordinarily natural fit: an interstellar guitar-woofing Black Yank set loose upon the faux-aristocratic British rock culture of the '60s. Not to mention its white women—at a time when America could find the Sidney Poitier vehicle *Guess Who's Coming to Dinner* a provocative and breakthrough portrayal of integrated romance.

Hendrix was not the first Black American male to take loads of white women to his bed, but he was the first one for whom that was read as a positive attribute by his white male fandom. Let's let Lewis "Flip" Barnes, whose whitey-hating cousin Stevie hammerlocked him into catching Hendrix live, chime in here. Barnes relates how "at the show it blew my mind to see these same redneck racist white boys who liked to call me all kinds of nigger and wanted to lynch my ass in Virginia Beach just gawking at Hendrix like he was god. I'm saying they acted like they would have given their girlfriends to Hendrix if they could have."

Unlike his older contemporaries Sidney Poitier and Sammy Davis, Jr., Hendrix never became the target of psychotic white male animus because he "fucked white," as the saying went. The pains with which other Black performers went to keep their liaisons with white women on the downlow back then never had to cross Hendrix's mind. The abuse, harassment, and bomb threats Sammy Davis, Jr. faced for daring to kiss a white woman onstage in 1965 make Hendrix's honorary-white-penis status come 1967 all the more startling. As antiquated as this all seems now (especially in light of Jerry Springer shows where "thug-niggas" routinely appear with two or more young pink gals vying for their charms), Hendrix overturned the most tragedy-laden of

American taboos by showing up with a blaring phallic symbol and baring it longer, louder, and lustier than his paler counterparts. (The matter-of-factness with which this taboo is treated on Springer also speaks to how under late-stage capitalism what was once the most unthinkable of acts can become commonplace and commodifiable in a heartbeat—easily the subject of another book.) Friends and roadies tell stories of Southern tours where promoters turned beet red at the sight of Hendrix, bevies of "Scandinavian-looking" Southern belles at his side, registering in hotels below the Mason-Dixon Line. According to vast anecdotal record (and can we go on record now and say Hendrix ranks as one of the most well-documented human beings to have ever lived), he was never threatened or accosted for these actions. This only a few scant years after the National Guard had to protect Black protestors who merely wanted to enroll at elementary schools and colleges in the region; this decades before the '90s, when Black ballplayers on the Boston Red Sox were being told by managers not to show up at local clubs with white women on their arms.

(Note, however, that in 1969 Hendrix was threatened by five hooligans who promised some Texas justice if he performed the National Anthem one night in Dallas. Says Rory Terry, "The leader got up in my face and said, 'You running this thing?' Jimi was standing right next to me but this guy didn't address him in any way. He said, 'Well you tell that fuckin' nigger if he plays the Star-Spangled Banner in this hall tonight he won't live to get out of the building.'" Hendrix pshawed, went on to Oh Say Can You See it in his own inimitable style, and nothing went down. Proof once again that the asshole who talks about setting some shit off ain't never the one you got to be worried about.)

Logic tells us Hendrix got special "exceptional Negro"-cum-"honorary white" treatment from whites because he was not perceived as a political threat (at a time when Black political threats seemed to be everywhere)—traveled in white company, drew a white crowd, kept a white band, and, oh yeah, bedazzled the Hostiles in a field considered a white man's province.

Hendrix was consciously (and some might say unconscionably) marketed to the world as if he were not Black. A whole mess of Black and white folk who should've known better bit the bait. But his slick, shadygrady manager Michael Jeffrey, we're told, correctly realized that if Jimi never talked about being Black, nobody else, Black, white, or indifferent, would notice it much either. This strategy worked fine until Hendrix woke up and smelled the alienation. By all accounts Jeffrey was never happy with him bringing brothers Buddy Miles and Billy Cox into his band or pursuing jazz interests with the likes of Miles Davis, Gil Evans, and Rahsaan Roland Kirk.

A number of things surely converged to make Hendrix rethink his relationship to other African Americans—the unavoidable turn racial conflict took in the country especially after King's assassination in 1968, the aggressive interest the Black Panther Party took in him as a possible cash cow for their multiple legal defense needs (showing up backstage at concerts, rolling mob-deep, trying to shake him down), and the return of a host of Black friends into his musical life like The Twins, Miles, his Army bud Cox, and percussionist Juma Sutan, among others.

In the summer of 1969 Hendrix decided to spend a couple months in Woodstock playing with mostly Black musicians before the Woodstock Festival. After which came the formation of his all-Black power trio, Band of Gypsys, whose triumphant New Year's Eve gig of that year changed the sound of soul music forever. The jury remains out as to whether Hendrix punked out on continuing the group after that show when various problems arose (not least being the lacing of bad acid into teetotaler Billy Cox's punch bowl), or whether his management manipulated its demise. Every Black Icon has her cross to bear and a defining time of crisis. For Hendrix that moment may have arrived with the Band of Gypsys debacle, about which there'll be more later.

As martyrdom-worthy Black Icons go, Hendrix fits the mold as readily as King or X. Like those juggernauts he was someone who defied stereotype, convention, and the easy road ahead to guide his people—all his chosen people—toward his version of the promised land, even at cost to his own stability and sanity. In music he proved himself quite the charismatic leader as the changes he wrought on jazz, blues, and rhythm and blues—sartorially, musically, and culturally—are still being felt, if vaguely understood, by lots of other Blackfolk.

The deal is this: For all that is inherently different, Other, romanticized, and exoticized about people of African descent and for all our questionable status as a signifier of primitivism and all that is humanly lacking in Anglo American culture, African American culture can be very conservative when not outright reactionary when it comes to embracing radical change. If Hendrix is a Black Icon, he is also a destabilizer of Black Masculine stereotypes from both within and without African American Culture. Hard where the culture says soft (the volume level of his guitar), relaxed where the culture says either "ghost" or fly into a rage (when among mobs of whitefolk). For this reason I consider him a supersignifier of Post-Liberated Black Consciousness. Someone who tried to show by example what life as a Black Man without fear of a white planet might look like, feel like, taste like.

A polemical addendum: Because there exists no so-called modern Black radio format actually hip enough to program Hendrix, our man remains a stranger in his own musical land. A situation made shamefully absurd by the fact that today's Blackpop, drenched in electronically manipulated funk, wouldn't sound like jack had Hendrix never existed. Here we have an immensely influential Black artist who transmogrified the flesh of Blacksound and yet somehow has no place among the stars or airwaves that dare call themselves Black. Were this not a culturally segregated society where Black people must have their apartheid-oriented radio stations and white people theirs, Hendrix's exclusion from the American Bantustan broadcasting system wouldn't matter. But Hendrix figures too prominently in the Blacksonic scheme of things for us to allow this sorryass state of affairs to go by without getting the gas face.

BLACK GUITAR SCIENCE

Hendrix obliquely falls into the ranks of The Great African American inventors—those boatloads of African Americans holding patents to such mainstays of modern life as the traffic light and the third rail (like my man Granville Woods). If we stretch our understanding of inventions to take into account guitarist John Scofield's notion of the blues as a great American invention, Hendrix was the electric guitar's Einstein if not its Edison, redefining the axe's sound spacially and temporally, universalizing the thing's applicability to any musical situation, and patenting more modern uses for it than anyone before or since.

In the recording studio and in tandem with superbly attentive engineers Eddie Kramer and George Chkiantz and electronics effects-pedal wizard Roger Mayer, Hendrix forever altered the expressive properties of the instrument. Beneath his fingers it became an orchestral baton latent with symphonic conjurings. To hear his multitracked studio version of the "Star-

Spangled Banner" is to realize anything the Boston Pops could do with the song, Hendrix could do with his bare hands. Long before he'd gotten to England and stumbled upon Kramer and Mayer, Hendrix had from all reports discovered the degree to which maximum volume extended the guitar's presence and palette as a lead instrument. Pernell Alexander, a musician buddy from his teenage years, declares, "Forget all those stories about Jimi discovering electronic sound distortion in New York or London. The truth is he discovered it here in Robert Green's basement. One of the amplifiers blew a tube, so we were playing with distorted sound . . . we had it overloaded."

Michael Bloomfield, guitarist for Paul Butterfield and Electric Flag, heard Hendrix in 1965 at the Café Wha? when he performed under the group name Jimmy James and the Blue Flames. "That day, in front of my eyes, flying missiles were going off—I can't tell you the sounds he was getting out of his instrument. He was getting every sound I was ever to hear him get right there in the room with a Stratocaster, a Fender Twin Reverb amp, a Maestro Fuzz Tone, and that was all. He was doing it mainly through extreme volume. How he did this, I wish I understood. I have never heard a sound on a Hendrix record that I have not seen him create in front of my eyes."

Feedback—the shrill, ear-damaging noise that occurs when an amplifier's signal overmodulates—became for Hendrix a means of expanding the instrument's sustaining capacity, as a violinist does with her bow or a horn player with her breathing. Nearly every piece of sound-enhancing gear available in a modern recording studio has been devised to emulate some musical effect of Hendrix's. The lyrical, composerly ways he laced his songs with such staples of contemporary pop as flangeing, phasing, chorusing, multitracking, pitchbending, tapesplicing, looping, delay, reverb made them register as far more than novelties and "ear candy" (that handy studio rat name for those sonic tricks meant to impress the world with what clever boys we are). Hendrix made all such devices and conceits emotional landmarks in his songs, largely because he privileged emotional projection as much as he did innovation. The acoustic blues tradition, of which Hendrix was a devoted disciple, was the by-product of diligent musical research and cathartic need. The paradigm of uncanny musicality and uncaged feeling Hendrix followed had been established by Southern blues players like Blind Willie Johnson and Charlie Patton and jazz pickers like Charlie Christian and Lonnie Johnson decades before he was born.

In the alchemist Hendrix's lab, dross ear candy was magically spun into black gold, turning musical effects into orchestral cornerstones. Hence, Hendrix's effects get under our skins as soulfully as an Otis Redding shout or an Al Green moan.

Hendrix—and it can never be said enough given how rarely true this is of his emulators—was that rare virtuoso who was also a hummable, hook-laden melodist, deep musical thinker, and emotive obsessive. He prized gut reactions above the whoring of razzle-dazzle, and also never tired of ragging on younger players, and even Eric Clapton, about the heresy of inadequate rhythm guitar skills. To Hendrix, rhythm playing provided the ground control for those farflung leads.

Some of this was simply R&B band experience talking.

Paul McCartney marveled that Hendrix only needed two days after its release to learn "Sgt Pepper"; drummer Bernard Purdie recalls Hendrix learning King Curtis's whole set the first night he was onstage with the saxophonist's unit. Miles Davis was also amazed at the adeptness and agility of Hendrix's untrained ear whenever he demonstrated advanced musical concepts for him on the piano.

In Hendrix, then, we have someone whose judicious and juicy use of novel electronic devices was grounded in disciplined technique. Beyond that, it was also spiritually grounded. Hendrix had specific ideas about the way modern electronic pop music was supposed to sound, and intuitively knew how those sounds would stab or sink into the head, the heart, the human core. For all the improvisational content in his work, on stage or in the studio, Hendrix never gives us the impression that what happened at the most extreme ends of his craft was randomly arrived at or ever beyond his control. Like only the most phenomenal improvisers in jazz, Hendrix took the odd pleasurable accident as not just serendipity but as a way to embark upon a new line of inquiry, the intent being not merely to duplicate the shock-of-the-new aspect of the thing but to intensely lyricize it. Like Jackson Pollock, who rewrote the book on the beauty of spilled paint, Hendrix lived to transmute the accident into intention. Hendrix is where excessive volume, distortion, frenzied rhythm, and techno fever conjoin forevermore in the dialect of modern pop. No Hendrix, no punk, no house music, no hiphop, and certainly no electronica. The willful and skillful abuse of musical machines, an abuse far beyond what the builder intended, begins with him. You cannot easily separate song from sonic treatment in Hendrix—the deployment of electronically induced vomiting is always tuneful and incredibly well calculated. Engineer Kramer marveled that Hendrix knew how the solos he took against music played on a tape machine running backward would sound when run normally.

If we praise Hendrix as a guitar-slinging Rosetta Stone, we no more than scratch the surface of his heraldic, innovative wizardry and contribution to twentieth-century culture. Yet if we continue to unpack his part in rewriting the all-American race game we see less a Martin Luther King figure than a Silver Surfer—a wounded and starcrossed creature consigned to live among us and further complicate such already big cosmological and ontological riddles as Black Musicality, Black Science, Black Identity, Black Esthetics, Black Iconic Being.

In this world Black Icons must do the work of powerful white cultural institutions. In the words of free jazz pianist Cecil Taylor, each man must become his own academy. Meaning the task of those figures we tag the Black Iconic Genius is to fill in all the gaps in memory, learning, and discipline that exist in African American culture because of the disruptions and discontinuities produced by that peculiar institution known as Slavery. These disruptions are most profound around the acquisition and transmission of cultural knowledge and worldly know-how. They are recorded in the forced and forcibly enforced command that African Americans disavow any understanding of the world that preceded the plantation.

Africans became African Americans when the language they sang, worshipped, fucked, and dreamed in became—after time, distance, and duress—not Bantu, Swahili, Yoruba, Ga, Ashanti, Wolof, Arabic, or Dogon but English. The African in them, though, was not so easily eradicated by lashing their tongues to Latinate syntax. What the scholars like to call African Retentions—profound cultural survivals and transmissions— wouldn't stop beaming black hole energy into these newly minted African Americans' sociocultural DNA. In enough of a rudely fractured, staggered, and static-filled form to ensure that in the less policed areas of our ancestors' captive humanity—their dance, song, wit, athleticism, ritual, and to some extent black-smithing and building craft—African ancestry shone through, kept on keeping on, to paraphrase Sister Gladys Knight, and came to define the American contribution to world kulcha.

Because the cosmology of African cultures refuses compartmentalization, heeds no categorical imperatives, needs no Cartesian solder to link thinking and being—because it can, in fact, speak of divine things and chew mundane bubble gum at the same time—a kind of African holography emerged, ensuring that a little byte could go a long way, and computate telemetry for the long road ahead, in effect catalyze the metamorphoses that would be required for the resilient Afrochip in the New World.

On the highest intellectual and artistic levels, Black culture does not merely produce novelists, thinkers, musicians, painters, poets. Due to the prehuman stigmata marking our skins, Black culture must produce demigods and mythological creatures: half-human, half-archangel winged things bent on saving the race, uplifting the culture, bearers of Black Redemption.

The culture tends to spit these types out as it sees fit. Whenever we need someone grand and mysterious to effect a shift in Black America's sense of prospect, prosperity, and possibility, then Shazam! here comes a Frederick Douglass, a Richard Wright, a Zora Neale Hurston, an Edward Kennedy Ellington, a Ralph Ellison, a Samuel Delany, a Stevie Wonder, a Toni Morrison. Many of them, like Hendrix, were autodidacts, disciplined, self-taught visionaries with a reverence for what Ellison meant when he talked about African American folk culture and all its symphonic possibilities. There is a note of dissatisfaction struck in the work of all these artists with easy assumptions about not just Black people, but about the American experiment (of which Hendrix may have been the most experimental exponent ever), and about even the very artistic mediums they've chosen to work in. They all convey a conviction that the novel or the swing orchestra or the folk tale or the science fiction epic or the guitar or Black feminism can be remade in their own image, remade to serve a higher calling, remade to speak their idiosyncratic tongues or serve their didactic, prophetic, Afro-futuristic ends.

Before Hendrix, and as far back as the prehistory of the blues, the guitar was understood as an accompanying instrument. When it became a jazz solo voice in the hands of people like Lonnie Johnson, Charlie Christian, and Django Reinhardt, it still never acquired the prominence as a jazz instrument of the piano or the brasses and reeds. In the hierarchy of jazz instruments horns are the royalty and guitar and vibraphone are maybe two steps away from being novelties. In country blues especially, the guitar's lingo evolved into a stunningly complex, shaded, and vocal tongue that could sing and solo with weight and authority in designated spots and sustain a piece without any vocals at all. What Hendrix did was effect a marriage or ménage à trois between the various strains of the blues, modern soul, avant-garde jazz, and the English rock and roll derivatives of same that pushed the guitar to the fore in a frightening way. Not until hiphop moved the sound of electronically altered drums to the fore would a single instrumental sound so flatten all other elements, including vocals, in a pop context. Not until technology provided a mechanism for digitized drum tracks to outshout guitars in the mix was the supremacy of the lead guitar solo as the voice of god in pop music sent packing. To some degree it is because guitar solos have become so irrelevant in modern pop that Hendrix looms larger than ever—one of the few electric guitarists still functioning on music's cutting edge. Hendrix invented the orgasmic rock guitar moment but was so much more concerned with song structure, lyrics, and textured sound than the vainglorious ejaculations that would come to define that arena staple of the '70s and '80s. The thing with Hendrix is that his rhythm guitar playing comes off as exciting and energizing as everybody else's best soloing. His rhythmic ability also made the line between a lead and rhythm guitar indeterminate if not superfluous. The call and response he often got going between the two approaches in a song rarely allowed for a clear line of priority or demarcation. By the time he gets to creating his own funk group, Band of Gypsys, he's leveled whatever supposedly distinguishes the roles of guitar, bass, and drums equally meaningless. . . . But we're getting way ahead of ourselves here. At this point less theorizing-cum-philosophizing and a few basic historical facts would now seem to be in order.

A BRIEF LIFE

James Marshall Hendrix was born John Allen Hendrix in
Seattle, Washington, on November 27, 1942. His first birth
name was given to him by his mother, Lucille, a rolling stone if
ever there was one. She gave birth while shacked up with a
reported slimebucket named John Allen while Jimi's dad, Al, a
Navy man, was stationed in Alabama. By the time Al got discharged and returned to Seattle, his son had been packed off to
Oakland, semi-adopted by loving strangers. This dereliction of
maternal duties, along with fastlife-loving Lucille's philander-
ing, caused a rift between mother and father that grew worse as
the years grew long. So severe became Al's antipathy toward
Lucille that when she died of tuberculosis in 1957, neither fif-
teen-year-old James nor his brother Leon were given consent to
attend the funeral. Jimi's mother and father did live together
for a short time after Al's return, but for most of her life James
would have to sneak off to see his sickly but sexually active

mother who would give up two daughters and another son for adoption before she passed away. The loss of his mother in life and then after death haunts many a Hendrix song, turning up obliquely in the lyrics of "The Wind Cries Mary," "Gypsy Eyes," and "Castles Made of Sand." It is also reflected in his lifelong desire for women to be his saviors, as can be heard in "Little Wing," "One Rainy Wish," "Angel," "Axis: Bold as Love," "Izabella," "Belly Button Window," and "Hey Baby."

Hendrix's parents were championship Lindy-hop/swing dancers. Al's parents, Nora Rose Moore and Bertran Philander Ross Hendrix, were Black vaudevillians who had migrated from Georgia and Ohio and retired from the road in the Vancouver/ Seattle area in the early 1900s. Hendrix seems to have come by his high-stepping showmanship and urban nomadism quite naturally.

Hendrix was strictly raised by his dad, a stern disciplinarian who did factory work before settling into a long career as a landscape gardener. He bought Hendrix his first electric guitar when Jimi was fourteen, after discovering that the broomstick straws he angrily found on the boy's bedroom floor had dislodged during some furious air-guitar sessions. Hendrix's obsession with playing guitar had actually began earlier and was so intense even at age eight that a school social worker concluded that denying him one might cause irreparable mental damage.

Contrary to popular belief Hendrix didn't turn spacey after one tab of acid too many—he was once asked by a grade school art teacher to paint three scenes and turned in a Martian landscape. Another friend remembers him at thirteen drawing on a classroom's wraparound chalkboard a kaleidoscopic mural of a Mexican village scene complete with big sombreros and palomino ponies charging out of the frame. Surviving watercolors he painted of the mountains around Seattle seem classically Japanese and may betray the influence of the Buddhist daycare centers fellow Seattle native Xenobia Bailey recalls Hendrix and herself attending as children.

By his mid-teens Hendrix had become one of the better rhythm and blues/rock and roll guitarists in the Seattle/Vancouver area. After two arrests for joyriding he dropped out of high school at seventeen and joined the Army. He went on to become a Screaming Eagle paratrooper in emulation of an older friend whose shoulder patch he'd admired. His training was done in Fort Campbell, Kentucky. After twenty-six jumps he attained the high rank of private, his own Screaming Eagle patch, and a broken ankle, which led to an honorable discharge in 1963. In the service he continued to practice like a fiend and to perform with local bands. His Army time was also responsible for his meeting bassist Billy Cox, who would later join him in Woodstock and help create his funkier post-Experience sound.

Once out of the Air Force, Hendrix became the quintessential rhythm and blues sideman, spending several starving and penniless years paying dues on soul music's infamous chitlin circuit. These years found him backing up King Curtis, Gorgeous George, and Little Richard and recording and touring with the Isley Brothers, who, much to their credit, didn't try to restrict his stagehog impulses. These were years where Hendrix also refined his penchant for such live blues staples as playing the guitar with his teeth, behind his back, between his legs, mid-somersaults, and so forth. These antics, along with a predilection for loud shirts and scarves (often tied around his knees and elbows), did not always endear him to employers like Little Richard, who felt upstaged. For his part Hendrix quickly grew tired of the late-to-bad-to-no pay that came with the illmatic chitlin circuit.

In 1965 Hendrix, broke as he would ever be, decided to come off the road and try to put his own act together in the West Village club scene that had nurtured his songwriting and vocal inspiration, Bob Dylan. In 1966, while performing with a quartet in the Café Wha? under the name Jimmy James and the Blue Flames, he was brought to the attention of Chas Chandler. The newly retired bass player for British Invasion rock group the Animals was looking for talent to manage. Suitably impressed by Hendrix (especially his version of "Hey Joe," a song Chandler thought could be an instant hit in London), he packed Hendrix off to England and helped put the original Experience together. The unit came to consist of Hendrix, guitarist-turned-bassist Noel Redding, and jazz rock drum pioneer Mitch Mitchell. The group was slowly introduced to the burgeoning rock aristocracy of the day. The Beatles, the Rolling Stones, Eric Clapton, and the Who took to him as one of their own. All were floored when not slayed when not sent into jealous hissy fits by Hendrix's skill, stage presence, sexual charisma, and originality. In 1973's *A Film About Jimi Hendrix*, Pete Townsend relates how he and Eric Clapton became fast friends upon Hendrix's arrival, and then un-befriended when Hendrix went back to America. British women of all ages were also said to be charmed to no end by Hendrix's humility, humor, and exquisite manners, the product no doubt of his father's home training and his innately friendly and seductive personality.

When the group's first full album, *Are You Experienced*, came out in 1966, the Jimi Hendrix Experience moved immediately to the front of the class of British rock acts. America loomed, and the group, recommended by no less a devotee than Paul McCartney, found its perfect breakthrough gig at the 1967 Monterey Pop Festival. There the Experience was introduced by Hendrix's good friend, Rolling Stone Brian Jones. This event found them sharing the bill with Otis Redding, the Who, Janis Joplin, and Ravi Shankar (who later said he liked Hendrix's music but found his stage antics obscene and his destruction of his instrument nearly blasphemous). The well-known D. A. Pennebaker documentary of that performance shows Hendrix, gingerly conked hair looking like a mess of black flames, sporting a ruffled shirt, a short military jacket, and skintight psychedelic red pants. True to chitlin circuit form he tosses his axe about like a rubber doll and eats her out while performing a set comprising a disparate mix of Howling Wolf's "Killing Floor," a revision of B. B. King's "Rock Me Baby," his own "Can You See Me," the Troggs' "Wild Thing," and Bob Dylan's "Like a Rolling Stone." Feedback, controlled yet untamed, was the order of the day. The set's career-making sacrificial climax found Hendrix fucking his scream-bloody-murder guitar against the speaker cabinets, setting it aflame with a butane lighter, then bashing it to bits before tossing the charred and splintered neck (sold at auction by Sotheby's for mucho dinero) out into the audience. The Experience had arrived.

In between a rigorous helter-skelter, cross-continental tour schedule the group found time to record a second studio album, *Axis: Bold As Love*. Released in 1967, it would yield several coveted and oft-covered Hendrix chestnuts: "Little Wing," "If Six Was Nine," "Up from the Skies," "Spanish Castle Magic," and the starbound title track. On both Experience records Hendrix's superb rhythm guitar supports lead work that embellishes the panoramic soundscape genius of Hendrix and Kramer. On that album especially, Hendrix and Kramer went all out to present the electric guitar as a mutant creation of nature and science fiction fantasy via various tricks of the trade by which the axe came to speak a mindwarping tongue. That tongue whizzed and whooshed about listeners' cerebellums like strafing flying saucers, or rattled and mesmerized them with the sound of the earth being downsized by deathray divebombs.

The Experience's touring schedule rose in 1968 to nearly 200 dates a year. Somehow, someway, Hendrix never got so toured out or partied out that he couldn't record for hours on end. By way of stamina and preternatural focus and drive he completed writing and recording his magnum opus, the four-sided *Electric Ladyland*. The album contains two versions of his autobiographical blues praisesong "Voodoo Chile"—a long slow jam-band version with a scroll of mythopoeic verses that would surely give any Wu Tang Clan member a run for their loquacity, and a second "Voodoo Chile (Slight Return)," which is faster, crunchier, and more lyrically concise, sporting what remains, hiphop notwithstanding, one of the more self-aggrandizing lyrics in human history (Jimi talking about how he's going to stand up next to a mountain, chop it down with the edge of his hand, then take the pieces and make an island, maybe even raise a little sand).

On *Ladyland* Hendrix lets the world know in no uncertain terms his mastery of every style of modern guitar playing and songwriting—jazz, blues, country, soul, rock—and the inventive variations and expansions he could wring from them all. The album's aquatic suite, "1983 . . . (A Merman I Should Turn to Be)" tracks as the origin of all subsequent ambient music. The progressive soul ballad "Have You Ever Been (To Electric Ladyland)" updates Curtis Mayfield for the age of *Star Trek*. Of *Ladyland's* many treasures the most beloved may be Hendrix's version of Bob Dylan's "All Along the Watchtower." (The lovefest extends even to the gnarly Dylan himself who now considers his own concert renditions of the song to be, strangely enough, a tribute to Hendrix. Dylan has also wondered aloud why Hendrix didn't do more of his songs as "They were all his anyway"—a case of the teacher humbling himself before his most apt pupil if there ever was one.) *Ladyland* became an instant chart-topper upon its 1968 release. But the incessant touring coupled with Hendrix's increasingly fanatical desire for perfection in the studio drove a wedge between him and manager/producer Chandler and bassist Redding, who both preferred the wham-bang in-and-out of the band's earlier sessions. The original Experience disbanded after months of rumors in late 1968.

Increasingly aware of his isolation from the Black community, Hendrix spent the summer of 1969 jamming with an expanded repertoire of musicians from the jazz, Latin, and soul worlds in a rented house in upstate New York. A more compact version of these experimental ensembles would perform with Hendrix at the Woodstock Festival of August, where he would unleash another instant classic in the form of his "Star-Spangled Banner." This interpretation is now generally understood as the battle cry and chief elegy for the '60s youth rebellion.

That uprising, led by the anti-war movement, the Yippies, and the Black Panthers, was one Hendrix seemed to have admired from afar with his wary, distanced artist's eye. On at least two reported occasions he was accosted backstage by members of the Panthers out to hit him up for cold cash money. In conversation with various reporters about race issues, Hendrix—never much of a "color-talker" according to his friends The Twins—proffers a muddle of opinions. These seem perfectly in tune with a man having to think on his feet about a subject he would have rather avoided:

"Music is stronger than politics. I feel sorry for the minorities but I don't feel a part of one. And I think the answer lies in music. One of the worst statements people are making is no man is an island. Every man is an island and music is about the only way we can really communicate."

"The race problem is something crazy. The Black riots in American cities that you read so much about in the papers currently are crazy. What they are doing is irresponsible. I think that we can live quietly, side by side. With violence, a problem like that has never been solved. The race problem exists in Europe too. But they don't talk so much about it."

Through reformed relationships with Black New York friends like The Twins, Hendrix became aware of his distance from the African American community. Another friend, the late Velvert

Turner, recalled Hendrix testily asking him after one show how many Blacks and Puerto Ricans he saw out in the audience.

Coinciding with Hendrix's growing desire to reconnect with Blackfolk came a rude blessing in wack-ass disguise: an outstanding contractual obligation from his starving artist past required recording a live album for Capital instead of his parent company, Warner-Reprise. The Band of Gypsys, as the trio of Hendrix, Cox, and drummer Buddy Miles came to be called, was the first all-Black rock power trio anybody had ever heard of. Their superfunky eponymous album would become Hendrix's most popular with African American audiences upon release and his most readily dismissed by white writers and fans. Its immediate embrace by Blackfolk is thanks to the booty-bouncing power of "Who Knows" and the twelve-minute anti-war requiem "Machine Gun," whose supernatural flow of ideas has found Hendrix favorably compared to John Coltrane on more than one occasion. The BOG's bizarre breakup after just one gig would spur a contentious debate that continues to this day as to whether Hendrix's management was threatened by his movement toward Black folks or whether he himself didn't want to continue sharing the stage with good brother but fellow singer Buddy Miles. The notion that management conspired to destroy the group before it could stare down white rock supremacy looks mighty attractive. More plausible though might have been a fear of the feisty Miles questioning what management was doing with all of Hendrix's money. (An informed debate between various parties, including The Twins, Miles, manager assistant Trixie Sullivan, road manager Jerry Stickells, and Black rockers Vernon Reid, Slash, and Lenny Kravitz, can be found on the DVD *Live at the Fillmore East*, which his estate released a few years ago.)

Soon after BOG's unraveling, Hendrix began work on another double LP, *First Rays of the Rising Sun*, which would be released posthumously as two albums, *The Cry of Love* and

Rainbow Bridge. Both were completed under the loving hands of Mitch Mitchell and Eddie Kramer in Electric Lady, the studio Hendrix had built in the West Village as a haven. Though it officially opened just a month before he died, it has since gone on to house major projects by Stevie Wonder and Led Zeppelin and, more recently, D'Angelo and the Roots.

Hendrix's death on September 18, 1970 (originally thought to be by asphyxiation due to an accidental overdose of sleeping pills and mishandling by paramedics; later determined by a second coroner's inquest two decades later to have been from (a) a dangerous overdose of foreign sleeping pills recommended by his German girlfriend Monika Danneman, (b) a suspicious gallon or so of red wine in his stomach, and (c) paramedics called to the scene far too late) brought to light discrepancies about his finances, which were investigated by lawyers for his estate. Their findings concluded that millions of dollars had been laundered through some Cayman Island tax shelters at the behest of Hendrix's manager, the former British Intelligence operative and all-around Shady Character, Michael Jeffrey. This man, who some have suggested had Hendrix killed because his contract with the guitarist was set to expire at the end of that year, died two years after Hendrix in a plane crash near the mountains surrounding his home in Majorca.

Hendrix, never a joiner, was generationally part of a group of experimental pop musicians, led by Dylan and the Beatles, who helped redefine music and politics, but refused membership in anybody's camp but that of musicians. Even among the other rock stars, though, Hendrix was, as Germaine Greer once pointed out, an outsider, being Black and a homeless American.

In America he was not a card-carrying street-fighting man of the ghetto, nor was he any longer part of the rhythm and blues world or the jazz world. The breakup of the original Experience in late 1968 led him to spend much of the first half of 1969 searching not only for new music and new musicians but attempting to create his own ad hoc community of multiracial freaks. He was also trying to establish a lot of distance from the image of him that the pyrotechnic Monterey Pop performance had fused into the public mind. He claimed that he was tired of being a clown and wanted respect for his musicianship. It was not an artistic stance without political undertones—especially in light of Robert Christgau's prescient review of the Monterey show where the critic decided Hendrix and his grinning gums, feather boa, and torched guitar heralded the arrival of a "psychedelic Uncle Tom."

The definition of an American, says writer Peter Schjeldahl, is someone obsessed with race. The African American negotiation of that obsession to positive benefit is a game that has been played since before the *Mayflower*.

The Minstrel tradition came about as one response to a basic need, currying white favor for security and social advancement. The well-organized and intricately plotted, easily betrayed slave revolts of Nat Turner, Gabriel Prosser, and Denmark Vesey could be described as another. Fight or flight has long been the modus operandum of the African captive in America—though fighting did not always mean a suicidal bare-knuckle contest against one's better-armed adversary, who, as poet Sterling Brown once put it, do not come in ones or twos but in tens. By the same token, Flight did not always mean toward freedom but sometimes away from one's humanity to the castrated sanctity of the minstrel's mask—a self-denying corridor of the soul so abysmal that success was judged by how well a brother came out on stage, in front of a room full of whites, in blackface with a watermelon on his grin.

Hendrix ultimately found a third option, more slippery and elastic, more trickster-like in its inversions of racial stereotyping. It allowed him to court white people without pandering to them and to intimidate them without raising the spectre of violence except by flashing his superlative, supernatural, musical chops.

If we had to give his gambit a name it would be Total and Complete Mastery of his Field. (Current exemplars would be Tiger Woods and Serena Williams.) There's a saying in the Black Community that a Black person has to be three times better than any white man to even get his foot in the door. Hendrix raised the requirements exponentially by being ten times better than anyone, Black, white, or Venusian, who ever lived, in the rock star–rock guitarist category. Generally speaking, such hyperbole, fine for newspaper reviewing, is wack between covers, but with Hendrix what's there to argue about? Who could argue that any of his competition doesn't pale by comparison? Or that he refuses not to be as enthralling to us now as he was then?

Hendrix's achievements in just four grueling and hyper-productive years between 1966 and 1970 still astound in their quantity and quality. His reach into our own time and the continuing contemporaniety of his sensibility three decades on suggest that unlike Elvis, Jimi Hendrix may never have to leave the building.

8

THE BLACK WOMAN'S GUIDE TO JIMI HENDRIX

Shango's complex artistic embodiments—warrior and lover, "water by the side of fire at the center of the sky," "I have an assassin as a lover"—extend back to antiquity. As early as 1659 Shango's upsurge into the world had been stylized by particularities of sculpture—the fertilizing thrust of the thunderstone into the earth indicated by an image carved in wood, pointing to his penis with one hand while indicating the source of that energy by pointing to the sky with the other hand.

Robert Farris Thompson, *Flash of the Spirit: African and African American Art and Philosophy*

There is no more vehement or energetic spirit. When a devotee is mounted by the spirit of Shango, he charges three times, head leading, spinning like a ram, towards the drums. Then he opens his eyes to abnormal width and sticks out his tongue, to symbolize a fiery belch of flames, and raises his thunder-axe on high and clamps his other hand upon his scrotum.

Fernando Ortiz, *Los Bailes y el Teatro de los Negroes en el Folklore de Cuba*

Hendrix's guitar seemed to be an extension of his body; the peculiar positions from which he sometimes played seemed a result of emotion—as if just to hold the guitar could not express his erupting feelings. The impression was that if Hendrix were to have put down his guitar, the music would have to come from his body—that the instrument was entirely superfluous.

Janie Gressel, *Seattle Post-Intelligencer*, 1969

Hendrix's legitimacy as a musician and composer, but also as a Black man and even as a sensual being, has been thrown into question by some commentators. In the provocative Band of Gypsys documentary produced by his estate, race clouds the air like a stank stygian mist. Heads can be heard going back and forth over whether his music was Black and whether he was even more down with Us than Them. Similarly, in some published accounts his sexual appetites and attitudes toward women are often reduced to no more than the typical carnivorous lust of the average touring rock star for hotyoungpinkgroupieflesh. As it turns out, the relationships he had with women were not just of the whambam variety, but varied, complex, and fraught with emotional tension.

Who knew? Not I, says the flyguy, until the brilliant 1973 documentary produced and directed by Joe Boyd and John Head came our way. In that film, Hendrix was unveiled as someone with many incredibly insightful, mature, and liberated women in his camp of various national origins and ethnicities. One of them was feminist author and activist Germaine Greer, reviled as a cliché pro-femme ballbuster in her time. Yet, when speaking of Hendrix's isolation and alienation in the rock pack, Greer sounds tender, motherly, and strangely guilt-ridden. "Well, he was a Black man in a white man's world, there's no doubt about that. It's an extraordinary sort of uptight white hetero set, the rock and roll set. They're all so aggressively normal with their wives and children and houses in the country. And he doesn't belong to that. . . . I put it down in a general sort of way to the impotence of the community he played for. We had no way of making him understand what he meant to us. He knew what the press thought, but he didn't know how much we needed him or what kind of energy he was giving us."

His longtime Harlem-based girlfriend Faye Pridgeon is also introduced to the world in the film as the uber-Amazon she is. Her recollections of Hendrix scuffling to get a break at Harlem jam sessions and playing Bob Dylan records at a volume near guaranteed to get them evicted are priceless. In a print interview from the period she provides the definitive words on Hendrix as a sex partner:

"Jimi loved fooling around with his guitar in bed and he always slept with it. I used to think of my competition not as a woman, but as a guitar. Many times he fell back asleep with it on his chest. Any time I tried to remove it he woke and said, 'No, no, no, leave my guitar alone!' All our activity took place in bed. He was well endowed. He came to the bed with the same grace a Mississippi pulpwood driver attacks a plate of collard greens and cornbread after ten hours in the sun. He was creative in bed too. There would be encore after encore, hard driving and steamy like his music. There were times when he almost busted me in two, the way he did a guitar on stage."

On the blunt, grunt-and-groan physical level nothing else need be added (I mean, *really*).

If we want to continue to discuss Hendrix's sexual charisma on a more spiritual level, though, we may need go elsewhere—to women who weren't necessarily his lovers, to some in fact who were barely out of diapers when he passed away.

A high-rolling trinity of women were not far from Hendrix in his final New York years: former Playboy bunny and reputed rock supergroupie Devon Wilson; Betty Davis, then Miles Davis's 23-year-old wife (already a hit songwriter for the Chambers Brothers and later to be a pioneer funk 'n' roll artist in her own right); and Colette Mimram, business partner of Stella Douglas, who was wife of Hendrix's friend, producer, and future Hendrix-estate administrator, Alan Douglas. All were thought by Carlos Santana to have had an enormous influence on both Hendrix and Miles. Betty Davis introduced Hendrix to Miles, while Wilson insinuated herself into Hendrix's life as sometime lover, recording organizer, and overprotective when not invasive social secretary. In his notes for the boxed set of *Bitches Brew*, Santana wrote fondly of these bitch-goddess-diva muses: "Around that time Miles always seemed to be in the company of a group of women some of us called the cosmic ladies. . . . You could see how these ladies were affecting Miles. They changed the way he dressed, the places he went and the music he listened to. Largely because of their influence Miles really began to check out James Brown and Sly Stone and he started hanging out with Jimi. I have always thought that *Bitches Brew*, the album, was, in its own way, a tribute in Miles' language to those women who opened his eyes to a whole new world and encouraged and prodded him to take that next big step."

The Velvet Underground's Nico, speaking after Hendrix's performance at the Monterey Pop Festival, proclaimed him "the most sexual man I ever saw on stage. Even Mick Jagger said so. It was not all the vulgar things he did with his guitar, though I enjoyed it when he burned his guitar at the festival. It was his presence. He was like a cat. He moved elegantly for a man. He was suave."

Seeking to prove the eternal reach of Hendrix's erotic charms, I've taken the liberty of asking some of my own female friends to explain the sexual appeal Hendrix holds for them, though his last appearance in the flesh was thirty years ago. All of these sisters could be described as quintessential New York City flygirls—stylish, bookish, sensuous, supertalented, and indefatigably opinionated. Taken together their responses affirm the way Hendrix continues to arouse that most elusive and mysterious of erogenous zones—the (Black) female mind.

Something in the way he moved, pimped, coutured . . .

Michaela Angela Davis is a fashion and beauty editor for a major African American women's magazine. Her brief on the man finds Hendrix deserving of sexy kudos for "how liquid and languid he was, and how drippy that made him always seem. Like he was surrounded by a lot of water and could still set shit on fire—literally! He was also drippy without seeming soft or gay and that was because he was not afraid to embrace his inner pimp. The pimp is the one place in our culture that allows Black men to be glamorous without their masculinity being called into question. A pimp's clothes are couture, which means handmade—wide collars, ruffled cuffs, peacock-colored combinations, loud creamy shoes. The pimp is a purveyor of sexuality. Hendrix makes me, as a woman, jealous of how easy he made sexuality seem. His inner pimp also allowed him to have a harem of bad women around him hooking his shit up.

"I've never wished I could have fucked him, but I have wanted to fuck that feeling he was having when he played. I never wanted to fuck the feeling Mick Jagger was having—though Mick is cool 'cause he was chasing that feeling too—but watching Hendrix fuck those amps was some of the best sex I've ever seen. Watching those films isn't something I can do in front of a whole lot of people. It becomes almost pornographic to me then."

Actor Aunjanue Ellis, recently seen in the Blaxploitation spy spoof *Undercover Brother*, also gets turned on by Hendrix's attention to detail with respect to appearance. "What made Hendrix sexy was nothing grossly or overtly physical—it was his new growth. How his hair was half-straightened and half Afro. That and his nonconformity, and his quiet volatility, and the way he put his mouth on that guitar in a way that suggests so many things to me, that's what made him sexy."

"He had a fuck-me voice and a fuck-me guitar," says personal fitness trainer Pekti Miles. "Wish I was that guitar." (Anthropology professor Dana Davis also relates how she finds pictures of Hendrix's mouth gazing salaciously upon his guitar to be incredibly sexy.)

Coptic DJ Mutamassik, in customarily terse fashion, locates her answer in "his lyrics, man. Those butterflies and moonbeams. I mean, shit, I want somebody to come take me away on a dragonfly."

Screenwriter and essayist Lisa Jones has written for directors Spike Lee, Charles Burnett, and Gina Prince-Blythewood. Known for her quick wit, Jones retorted, "What do you mean what made him sexy? You mean besides him being a spaceman— all androgynous and masculine at the same time? Well, I also loved his speaking voice. The way he didn't seem to be in a rush to go anywhere but had a lot to say. He looked like he was always traveling. Like he had been somewhere you hadn't been. Men like those are the kind of men you want to know about, and curl up with, and listen to for a while. You can learn from them.

"I also appreciated that his band looked like him—like they were aspiring to his sexuality. Most of the time if there's a Black guy in a rock band, the white guys are the sexual ones with the long hair and the skinny waists. There was something very commanding about the way that was flipped in Hendrix's band."

Master chef, astrologer, witch, oracle, you name it, Stephanie Kelly compares Hendrix to rapper DMX in being "an animal in the way he set out to put Black people on the map in rock and didn't let anything or anybody stand in his way. That and his skill made him sexy."

Finally there is fine arts photographer and activist Jackie Terry, of the Witness Project on police brutality. "Hendrix," she gushes, "was my first crush. He projected possibility and limitlessness and a life without boundaries. That was all extremely sexy coming from a Black man at that time."

The inner pimp. The new growth. The butterflies, moonbeams, and the traveling by dragonfly. The spaceman androgyny. The life without boundaries. The breaking a woman in two the same way he did a guitar onstage. With responses like those it'd be hard for anybody not to comprehend Hendrix as sexy by proxy.

What continues to fascinate about Hendrix, given how entwined race and sex are in the anxious American psyche, is how his public preference for young white women never brought him the hatred and bomb threats white supremacists had lobbed at other Black male celebrities like Sammy Davis, Jr. only a few years earlier. Was it because Hendrix was so disconnected from the Black struggles of the time that he was perceived as an honorary white? Was it because of how he was enfolded into the race-mixed counterculture? Or was it because white boys revered him to such a god-like degree for his handling of their phallic symbol that he could do whatever he wanted with as many white girls as he wanted to? Because the truth is that no Black male has ever been as beloved by white men as Jimi Hendrix was. Not Miles Davis, not even O. J. Simpson.

Three Hendrix Poems by Krista Franklin

Tease

1.
he came to me at night
guitar sheathed as a condomed phallus
strap slung over
one yellow shoulder

sensing my attraction to fire
he raspy whispered
Ladyland *lore*

lured me with phrases
crackling in the spaces
between us

2.
he spread me
in twin bed of blues

tangled me
in sheets of poems
he pushed from my lungs
like a harp
pressed his
wanderlust fingers
deep in imagination's
openings

3.
remote as Pluto

he soldered me
into alloys of wants & wonts

steamed stanzas
from the heat of his mouth

word-played me
into a shuffled deck
of wildcards

"Crosstown traffic," Kent State Cafeteria, 1992

I'm listening

In the kitchen my pelvis pressed
against the edge of slick stainless

A familiar voice calls
on too-low radio

Guitar licks ebb among clanging pans
and raised voices

Cucumbers wait to be cut
half-filled plastic containers clutter table

My scalp tingles

There is something
elusive on my tongue

A name lost in memory

Groupie

Regard his body—

long plane of legs
the peak and slope
of fingers
still as stone,
tips tough as leather,
guide me to the cliffs of my body,
move me straight to center.

Strewn piñata treats:
twisted black panties
curl on the rug.
On the table, my
sterling cigarette holder;
a sea of dead butts,
my reflection.

On the bed,
his body turns
toward the sun like a dial,
morning filters the wilderness
of his hair, his mouth—
down-soft lips
slightly parted.

What a universe
behind thin skin.
What an orbit.

(TALKIN' ABOUT) MY JIMI HENDRIX EXPERIENCE

Strangely enough, I've never written about Jimi Hendrix before now.

I've certainly, in clichéd critspeak, dropped the odd reference to something as Hendrixian, but nothing on the man himself or his work. You would think that after twenty-five years of musing in print over various Black musical icons this wouldn't be the case.

For reasons yet to be divined neither the fates nor the furies have seen fit to bind us together before now. Certainly it has not been for lack of topical product to essay on in one of the rags I write for—*The Village Voice, Rolling Stone, Vibe, The New York Times,* to namedrop a few. Over the past quarter century the Hendrix legend has cattleprodded into being a small memorial library of biographies, hagiographies, graphic novels, critical reckonings, companions, almanacs, omnibuses, artist and photographer monographs, tribute albums, family albums, posthumous releases, remixes, repackaged remixed and remastered reissues, interview CDs, instructional tapes, bootlegs, concert films, a Showtime biopic, a new coroner's inquest, and now even a Frank Gehry–designed theme park/museum, the Experience Music Project, opened by Microsoft's Paul Allen in Seattle

If there is any twentieth-century figure who seems less in need of further prose assault from another blathering idiot about the meaning of his life, death, and music it would be our man James. But Hendrix After Death is a growth industry—a seemingly inexhaustible project with indefatigable entrepreneurial momentum, moxie, hustle, and drive. We simply did not get enough of this man while he was alive, and our insatiable appetite for him has ensured him a vigorous afterlife in our hypercapitalist hogheaven. (On the recording "Somewhere," he prophetically sang, "My mildew mixes with my dreams, / Can't even tell my feet from the sawdust on the floor. / Maybe they'll try to wrap me in cellophane and sell me, / Brothers help me, and don't worry about looking at the score.")

As it was for many African American males of my generation, *Band of Gypsys* was the first Hendrix album I acquired during the otherwise uneventful Summer of '71. A rite of passage among my Dayton, Ohio, homeboys was shoplifting the aforementioned album from the local mall. Whether intended or not it is still the Hendrix album whose detractors and devotees tend to split along racial lines. The reason Black people groove to it instantaneously is because it's got so much rumpshaker appeal going for it, courtesy of Billy Cox and Buddy Miles. And though everyone references "Machine Gun," as they should, as the definitive musical statement about the Vietnam War, you'd be hard-pressed to find an African American guitarist or bass player who does not, in spare moments, noodle over the very phonky riff for "Who Knows," which precedes it on the album. Both Vernon Reid's Living Colour and Me'Shell NdegéOcello's band have covered the intricate and inspirationally upsurging "Power of Soul" in their live concerts. Hendrix's solos on Miles's "Them Changes" and his own "Message of Love" are slinkier than anything he ever played with the Experience. Those who pan the album single out Miles's drumming for its heavyhanded consistency and note that even Hendrix thought Miles's screamin'-and-testifyin' vocals were a tad over the top. But the firmament provided by Miles and Cox's teamwork definitely pushed Hendrix's guitar playing into some novel places rhythmically, sonically, and emotively. "Machine Gun" is the culminating proof, a twelve-minute blues drone that reminded my grandfather of John Lee Hooker, and has provoked many others to hear an improvisatory display of will, imagination, and stamina comparable to the Coltrane of *Meditations* and *A Love Supreme*. The solo begins where most guitar solos climax, on a bawling high note that builds in pummeling, incantatory caterwauling fury from there. The song's climax, with its echoes of strafe bombs, remote control weaponry, and desiccated human cries, belies the effect of many other screaming Hendrix denouements. This time he offers up a preview of nuclear winter, an apocalypse of fire and ice, and because of how it's programmatically and thematically linked to making war not love, we hear something far more chilling than the stagy auto-da-fé he unleashed at Monterey only three years earlier. Lenny Kravitz once joked that after listening to "Machine Gun" he's usually so drained he has to go sleep for a week. For anyone who knows the piece, that statement hardly reads as hyperbole.

Like many English-speaking males of my generation—those born between 1945 and 1965—Hendrix and puberty came into my hands at roughly the same time and hit with about roughly the same force. Unlike many of my adolescent enthusiasms

Hendrix has not withered or shriveled with age. Quite the opposite—he keeps pace with the various au courant enthusiasms that I've acquired along the way to middle age—musical and otherwise. Decades later, Hendrix's art refuses the dustbin of nostalgic reverie or the obsolescence proposed by such new wrinkles as drum-and-bass, hiphop, triphop, and techno. Largely because of his willful way with guitar stompboxes and the ghosts haunting his machines, he seems a contemporary of today's laptop abusers, a sagacious prophet of the glitch in ancestral, hippyfied trimmings. Not even the necessary and merciful demise of the guitar as the penultimate pop phallic symbol has dimmed the houselights shining from the shrine of Hendrix. Though the déclassé genre known as cockrock was largely, and inadvertently, a Hendrix invention, Hendrix continues to live on in our turntablists and digital sampler devotees because of how he charged his electronic tools—not how he displayed them. Hendrix gave his high-watt animals tongues and made them speak, scream, screech, whine, sigh, shout his name when spanked, scrawl his fame on heavenly toilet stalls, and so forth and whatnot.

And can we talk about Noise? If Noise is the spook who sits by the popular jukebox, Hendrix remains that Casper's head shaman, conjurer, conqueror, warrior-poet, and worldly champion. This is after all the man who gave Noise license to ill in top-forty music, and for that Noise is forever grateful. If Noise is the fancy of the art-music muse, as she surely has been since Varèse, Hendrix remains her favorite little darling—with no slight intended toward fellow travelers Brian Eno, the Bomb Squad, the RZA, DJ Spooky, Tricky, Goldie, DJ Shadow, Nobekamu Takemura, Otomo Ishide, Timbaland, Vladislav Delay, Keino Haije, Acid Mothers Temple, Dan the Automator, and the Invisbl Skratch Piklz. All of whom learned from Hendrix's example that the noisy grain of their own voices could be magically coaxed, massaged, and released from their favorite piece of hotwired audio hardware.

Though great music usually speaks of its own time first and not even Hendrix's music is immune to showing its age, Hendrix remains a zeitgeist artist—a member in good standing to this very day of that house of common prayer the African American comedian Flip Wilson once described as the Church of What's Happening Now. Being a man for all musical seasons and all musical reasons, Hendrix is also one of those deceased musical legends who demand we question what it was like to confront his noise in the flesh—to have it run across your skin, surge through your synapses, gallop up your ganglions, sizzle and pop from the touch of its air-crackling electromagnetism, make you brace yourself before its high decibel count. (The faces who appear in the footage of Hendrix crowds are no help really—too high, too spoiled, too anticipatory in their desire for the clown prince of guitar-smashing fools to appear. They could be any other rock god's audience really, with responses ranging from the stunned to the staggered to the superficially enlightened to the seriously drugged, eroticized, aerobicized, clueless, indifferent—looking like anything in fact but the face of mass hysteria you'd expect.)

OK, yes, Hendrix did have less than transcendent moments on stage, more often than not if we set the bar by his own best performances. But because he was a master improviser and an irrepressible ham, his most memorable feats of derring-do and abandonment did serendipitously occur on stage as much as during his fabled anal-retentive studio visits. (How anal you ask? So anal that on *Axis: Bold As Love* and *Electric Ladyland*, Noel Redding would exit the studio for the local pub out of boredom as Hendrix tinkered on. Redding frequently returned to find that Hendrix, also a supremely proficient Jamerson/Motown-style bassist, had gone ahead and laid the bass parts down himself. The end of the Experience probably begins there.)

You would think that an artist so invested in the studio as a medium would lose something in the translation from tape-manipulated wizardry to the concert hall, but per Michael Bloomfield, Hendrix's warlock powers were in his fingers, not his gear.

Now that every electrified musician has some simulacrum of Hendrix toys for use on stage and in the studio we are still waiting to hear some intrepid and anointed child of god wring as much presence and surface beauty from the damn things. So much style and brio, as it were. None has come forward (though Prince has had his moments).

To speak on the presence of things not seen leads us to recognize that as a stylist Hendrix demands we start hearing him in terms of his voids as much as his volumes, his absences as much as his appearances, his natural gases as much as his vacuum-tubed and transistorized solids. Our old Russian friend Vladimir Nabokov believed that all a writer has to leave behind is her style—the discernment, flair, and discrimination that inform the artist's choices.

The idea that what he left out was as important as what he left in suggests Hendrix sculpted sound as Michaelangelo did marble, cutting away everything from the stone of rhythm-and-blues form that was not his David.

The clear craft that went into his recordings formed cacophonous and euphonious order out of the chaos of a sublime interior monologue where dreams of extraterrestrial surfaces bled into forlorn conversations with his dead mother. There is, then, a Zen of Hendrix. A Hendrix as comfortable with silence as with ultrasonics, the Hendrix whose life of the mind weighed as heavily on him as his meteoric rock star lifestyle. As Lisa Jones alluded, Hendrix was a quiet, confident man in conversation who had volumes ready to spill from his mouth given the properly attentive ear. Where you really get a sense of how he experienced the world of the mind is in his lyrics, which ranged wildly with respect to thematic content and whose empathy for the human comedy can only be described as novelistic.

There is, again per Ms Jones, something remarkably unrushed and lacking in urgency about Hendrix's speaking and singing voice—even on rock-hard numbers like "Spanish Castle Magic" and "Voodoo Child," he moves freely from the heatedly heroic to the coolly laissez-faire like it ain't nobody's business if he do. Who else has written songs where the narrator in one breath claims to stand up next to mountains and chop them down with the edge of his hand, then turns around, apologizes for taking up all your sweet time, politely declares he'll give it back to you one of these days, then provides the fillip of how if he don't see you no more in this world, he'll meet you in the next one, so don't be late? Foreplay, afterplay, sexplay, courtship, cocksmanship and seduction, violent penetration and volcanic eruption—Hendrix confuses it all in the paradoxically tight and porous spaces provided by his lyrics, his din, and his vocal delivery.

If his lyrics are mad-thoughtful (and very well thought out), his alternately soft-and-hard, purring-and-howling phrasing and projection of them seem even more strategic.

The advent of hiphop MCs (hands down the most musically intelligent interpreters of lyrics today) has made Hendrix's own conversational way with a line sound like even better singing than even we fans originally thought. In music it sometimes does take a marginal device like rapping becoming a (mainstream) artform in its own right before the musicality inherent in the practice even becomes evident.

Akin to Schoenberg and Webern in twentieth-century European concert music, Albert Ayler and Ornette Coleman ecstatically altered notions of legitimate pitch, rhythm, and dynamics in jazz, elevating things that were once considered the epitome of bad saxophone playing—excessive vibrato, squealy upper register squalls, hurried obbligatoes on ballads, crawling runs on uptempo numbers, and so forth. Like Hendrix, they unashamedly did damage to orthodoxy in a manner so loud, proud, and defiant that it became a new order of prowess—and one so transformative and enduring that nowadays not even the softest of commercially viable soft-jazz hacks seem unruly if they slip an out-of-tune squawk or whinnying glissando into their ad-libs. Likewise hiphop has made rhythmatized speech, Black Talk by any other name, a musically and commercially successful American songform. In light of this, Hendrix's conversational crooning—inspired, various informants have told us, by Bob Dylan's early embrace of the talking blues form—now comes across as even more composed and structured than it was given credit for prior to the hiphop era.

Of course the rhythm and blues tradition Hendrix was grounded in as a journeyman player always privileged the singer who could, in supple fashion, leap from a whisper to a scream. There is always so much casual and even hushed conversation going on when we hear any of soul music's master vocalists—an Otis, an Aretha, a Marvin, an Al—deliver a secular heartache lyric back to the church. The conversational dimension of their craft too rarely receives tribute in accounts of classic soul.

Hendrix, who was such a screamer in his guitar, but hardly so Pentecostal from the throat, found his singing voice in a souped-up version of those close-up and personal frequencies. Frequencies We People Who Are of a Darker Hue associate with bluelight in the basement, winding and grinding sessions, and that subgenre of classic soul known as the slow jam. The song "Have You Ever Been (to Electric Ladyland)," his most lush and luscious rendering of the style, is a swooning and steamy paean to his two muses, electric music and electric Woman (yes, that's with a capital dub-ya, thank you).

Visions and dreams are where Hendrix lived more vividly than the rest of us, from available testimony. Never-never land was his virtual reality. Even before his mother passed away, he recollected working on his abandonment issues there in his REM phase: "My mother was being carried away on this camel, she's sayin', well, I'm gonna see you now, and she's goin' under these trees, and you could see the shade, you know, the leaf patterns across her face when she was goin' under . . . you know the sun shines through a tree and if you go under the shadow of a tree, shadows go across her face . . . green and yellow, and she's sayin', well, I won't be seein' you too much anymore, you know, I'll see you, and then about two years after that she dies, you know, and I said, yeah, but where are you goin'? I will always remember that."

If his Herculean musical labors can be said to have a purpose it was to transport the rest of us into his anguished dreamworld with him. "Sky-church" became the name he would give to his ministry and audio-visual quest, somewhat in jest, but somewhat not. Having voiced severe reservations about organized Christianity, Hendrix may have believed he had seen the real mountaintop and could Moses us all back through his music. Perhaps he felt he had a transformational duty to perform with his gift, making him kin in his own way to Martin Luther King, Malcolm X, Amiri Baraka, Muhammad Ali, and other potent figures of the day who felt called upon to deploy their charisma and creative powers to enlighten, redeem, and reduce the African American misery index.

Lofty ideals came with the territory back then—the Civil Rights and Black Power movements and anti-establishment, anti-war youth movements had made it so. Hendrix was, by dint of skin, lifestyle, and musical idiom, a representative of that idealism and, depending on who was checking him out, a potential symbol, benefit breadwinner, rabble-rouser, messiah.

Even before Hendrix properly unpacked his gigbag or had figured out how his music could serve humanity, the avant-garde saxophonist Albert Ayler had declared music the Healing Force of the Universe while John Coltrane had recorded his spiritualized masterpieces *Meditations* and *A Love Supreme.* Historically, these are important precedents for Hendrix insofar as they locate a devotional potential in semi-popular, secular music, and music conversant with the extremes of dissonant expressionism. The combined influence of the Hendrix and Coltrane devotional streams would in turn beget Devadip Carlos Santana and Mahavishnu John McLaughlin who, under the tutelage of their prefix-naming guru Sri Chinmoy, placed rock guitar in service to G-O-D on their collaboration *Love, Devotion, Surrender.* The Coltrane/Hendrix axis would also predispose many to the sonic syncretism proposed by reggae, Rastafari, and Bob Marley and the Wailers, whose Rasta Revival would chant Babylon in rock arenas everywhere. Hendrix also prepares the way for Prince, who like Little Richard and Jerry Lee Lewis before him would have us believe that Lucifer and Jesus were at war over a soul in his Hendrix-tinged rock and roll.

The cool thing about Hendrix was that he didn't seem to believe rock and roll needed a catechism or a church doctrine to perform the task of salvation. Just a voodoo chile, a Fender guitar, and a stack of Marshall amps would do fine, thank you. Few would argue with you if you said Hendrix was supernaturally inspired, since in his case the ratio of inspiration to perspiration, of serious preparation to serendipitous opportunity, appears to have been even. Where did he get his funk from? If we rang up George Clinton, would even he know? We might assume from the same treasure room all creative people gather theirs from. Only Hendrix seems to have stomped out of the joint hauling freight cars' worth of the stuff while the rest of us, Miles Davis and Jean-Michel Basquiat excepted, can barely fit our booty into nickel and dime bags by comparison. Where did he get his funk from? And how did he come by so much at the same time?

Unanswerable questions these may be, and far beyond this interlocutor's talents and grasp of the essential Mysteries. But like the salt-peter that cats in 'Nam said could make you a believer, Hendrix tells you that something else really is out there. For some of us Hendrix is the verifiable proof that this world contains far more than can be found in your calculations, Horatio. More than even the most rococo equations our most erudite mathematicians deploy to reduce the wonders of the universe to a chalkboard exercise.

Hendrix, we know, loved science fiction and, like Sun Ra, fully embodied what its devotees like to call the genre's grand sense of wonder—though he was committed to getting us all Out There quicker than NASA ever could. For this reason, probably, my absolute favorite lyric of his is the one that goes, "I make love to you in your sleep and yet you feel no pain because I'm a million miles away and at the same time right here in your picture frame." That's the Jimi Hendrix I fell in love with: Jimi as incubus. Jimi as dreamfucker. Jimi the randy starman with the sensory syrynx scarier even than the one Samuel R. Delany gives his Hendrixoid character Mouse in his novel *Nova*.

Fell in love as hard as others would fall for the Hendrix of "Machine Gun" or the Jimi of the "Star-Spangled Banner" or "Foxy Lady" or "Angel" or "1983 . . . (A Merman I Should Turn to Be)." We don't have to choose between them to wonder how so many selves got bundled up in one rail-thin guy. There is, of course, no one answer. So we shall, for our next trick, paint quite a picture, a Rod Sterlingesque tapestry, if you will, of how many sidepockets those selves flew in and out of. To do this, I'll need some help, a few friends to guide us as we backtrack around and about the dusty roads our troubadour traveled while he was an upright and walking blues man. Toward that end we have enlisted The Twins, Ronnie Drayton, Xenobia Bailey, and Craig Street—voices chosen not because they have the last word on Hendrix (as if such a thing could be even imaginable) but because they best suit our Racial Agenda: clearly marking Hendrix as a Black man with ties to several very disparate Black communities of the '40s, '50s, and '60s.

CAN I GET A WITNESS?

The Twins

I took to calling Arthur and Albert Allen "The Twins" before I knew that's what everyone called them. Hendrix fans know them best as the Ghetto Fighters, the name they recorded under on The Cry of Love, War Heroes, *and* Rainbow Bridge *albums. In* A Film About Jimi Hendrix *they make several riveting appearances before a Washington Square Park backdrop expounding on Hendrix run-ins with management, the Black Panthers, and Death. On the latter topic Albert memorably waxes on his "Alpha-Jerk theory" of Jimi's exit: "While the other type of sleep, the light sleep is coming upon you, there's two sockets where you can go into. One socket is death and one socket is the socket to live. I think they call that an 'alpha-jerk.' An alpha-jerk is—have you ever felt as though, 'Oh wow, I'm going into the wrong hole here'? And you really feel funny, like that's possibly the hole to die. And the other side is to go ahead and sleep and get into your subconscious and whatnot, which we normally go*

into. I believe that Jimi, possibly, could have got into his alpha-jerk field and it kind of felt groovy to him because he was high, slightly high, and he said, 'Damn, I'm Jimi Hendrix, I wonder if I can die?' And the alpha-jerk came on him, and he just said, Fuck it, let me try the alpha, and slipped on out. And . . . another way he could have died, I always felt, was, uh, dying out of pure frustration, just saying, you know, fuck it."

So impressive was this bit of philosophizing that when we met a decade ago at the Apollo Theatre I could not resist addressing him as the Alpha Jerk. Fortunately for me he took this rib in jest.

As far as anyone can tell the Twins were among Hendrix's best Black male friends and confidants. The story of how their lives inter-sected with Hendrix is also a microcosmic view of the social and politi-cal forces that ravaged Harlem as the mecca of African American society in the 1950s and 1960s. Anyone who has encountered them knows that in true telepathic twin fashion, they start and finish one another's thoughts. (You can play a piece of music through headphones to one brother and the other one will respond to verbal descriptions of the piece, looking as though he's the one caught up in the rapture of rhythm and rhapsody too.)

In the 1980s the Twins were briefly known as rhythm and blues duo the Aleems and scored a hit on their independent label Nia Records. Today they go by the handles Tundera and Taharqa reflecting a conversion to the ancient Egyptian or Khmetan spiritual practice of Ma'at. They are also self-employed weightlifters and nutritionists who do training programs and mentorship for a growing number of hiphop industry clients.

We were born on Valentine's Day. We were premature and they thought were going to die because we were seven-month babies and because our mother didn't know she was having twins.

Our mother is from Jacksonville, Florida, our father is from Tampa. They met in New York, had five children. We're the only twins and we're in the middle.

Our father worked for the railroads and was a member of the Brotherhood of Sleeping Car Porters. He had the utmost respect for the leader of that organization, A. Phillip Randolph. He expressed that respect to us on numerous occasions before we even knew what he was talking about.

Our mother was a musician, as was her mother. They were teachers, but they would never teach us. So most of our musical learning we had to do by ear.

It wasn't cool to teach men, from my mother's perspective. Things like teaching boys how to cook and how to play piano, having boys come into the kitchen—all of these things were totally off limits to us. My mother was a chauvinist. My mother was into women and for the girls. The boys had to fend for themselves. We were just there as slaves. We were slaves for the girls.

I think I remember a couple times hearing, Come here, Slave. We were Slave Number One and Slave Number Two.

They also trained us to take care of sisters. If we ever became successful we were told to make sure our sisters were taken care of. Our sisters grew up with that attitude. They were Black American Princesses.

As little kids we knew there was something wrong with that concept, but they were down with the matriarchal bullshit. We thought we were equal but uh-uh.

When we would have family singalongs our mother would orchestrate us and say, "Boys, sing this"—and it was always the inferior notes. It was good, though, because it taught us harmony.

Any negative situation we turned into a positive.

One of our sisters was a piano prodigy, so our mother put her in the hands of other instructors. Our job was to flank our sister on her way to lessons. Make sure she got to her destination. Then sit, read a paper quietly, and when she finished, bring her back. To escort and protect, that was our job. Thing was, our older sister was bigger than us and she could beat us up.

But a strange thing would happen when we would go with her to these lessons. She had a teacher that was very, very strict, almost violent. If this woman saw her hands get lax she would beat her hands unmercifully with a ruler. Tell her to straighten up her spine and whatnot. Our sister would be in there crying through those lessons.

They thought she was Carnegie Hall level. They would try to put her into this right posture. Our sister wasn't into that, so they would beat her. But she would be playing some of the most beautiful concertos and songs.

We would sit back and listen and memorize these things. We'd go home and start trying to learn them or ask my sister to teach us. She had become totally turned off by the lessons, but she loved us so much she would give us a few lessons.

Our mother of course objected to this. She'd say, "You're gonna turn those boys into sissies." One of her other sayings was "Stop banging on that piano." No matter what we did, she wanted our sister's touch. Our touch was too hard, she said.

So we'd say, "Teach us a soft touch."

She'd say, "Go play some baseball. Do something."

We had the nerve to tell our mother we wanted to go to Music and Art High School, and she was like, "What?" I think because of her failure in becoming a professional musician she wanted us to do something else.

Well, she failed to pursue her dreams in music because she got married, had children, then gave her life to her husband, and we were going to pay for that. We were the Getback. Yeah.

Eventually we began to extract what it took to understand music in spite of our mother. Unfortunately it took longer because we were learning by ear. But that was good. There were ups and downs to that. Music became like masonic teachings to us. The Mystery System.

One of the good things was that we came out of that with our own unique approach. We picked up certain techniques and scales and found that we could play anything by ear.

Our sister Alma found this fascinating because she could only play what she read from the score. She'd say, "How do you do that?"

We were fascinated that she couldn't play by ear.

❧

The '50s, when we were coming up in Harlem, was really an innocent period. We had a lot of good times.

Our block was on 141st Street between 7th and 8th Avenues—a brownstone block at the time. There were very few projects in Harlem at that time.

That area fostered a lot of talent. There was a hotel called the Woodside on Seventh Avenue and 141st Street. It's the same hotel Count Basie wrote a song called "Jumping at the Woodside" about.

Our father had an accident and lost his job with the railroad. He started drinking. One of the places he frequented was the Victoria Bar, which was part of the Woodside Hotel. Downstairs was a restaurant that many jazz masters frequented—Count Basie, Duke Ellington, Miles

Davis, Charlie Parker, John Coltrane. All of them would go to this hotel and so we got to see these geniuses.

There were older people who would school us as to who they were. Many times we would hear incredible music from them jamming together.

I think they dealt drugs inside the Woodside Hotel. When Ray Charles started coming around is when we knew they were selling more than marijuana because he was known as a heroin addict at that time.

Later on the new sound became doowop, as jazz was on the wane. On our block was Jimmy Castor who used to write for Frankie Lymon—who was everybody's idol.

In the 141st Street area there were several other top-notch doowop groups.

You also had people living in the vicinity like Sammy Davis, Jr. and the Isley Brothers, who lived on 142nd Street.

That area nurtured a very musical climate. It was very competitive but in a positive way.

We also had good professional fighters who came out of 141st Street, because there was a Catholic boys school. Ray Robinson and Vincent Shomo used to come around.

It was a very positive environment prior to the projects coming.

The first suspicion we had that there was something else going on in the world was through this old guy named Elmo who dressed Afrocentrically in the '50s. Elmo would tell us about people like Patrice Lumumba. His look was very different to us because all we knew about Africans was the bones in the nose. Elmo would come and tell us to be proud of our blackness. He was like a griot. He would tell all the kids about Africa, and the great men of Africa, like Jomo Kenyatta. He would make each and every one of us say their names. He embedded those names in us, and he would tell us to always look for those names.

This particular block was like a village. There were three parts of the block. The middle contained the Catholic church that we lived right next to. To the left side were the heathens, and to the right were the Baptists. We associated with all sides.

In that block there were four sets of twins, which was strange.

It really was like a village in Africa where everybody knew each other. Another beautiful thing was there were a lot of different kinds of spirits there. Like we'll never forget as kids seeing a woman knock a man's ear off with a bottle. All the kids just stood around looking at the ear.

We didn't know the ear could detach from the body.

There was a lot of closeness and comradery going on in the block.

But what happened was the Catholic church made a deal with the city to build projects that would have the monsignor's name on them. They, in turn, convinced everybody on the block this would be better for the community. They never predicted the destruction it would cause later on.

It was the worst thing that could have happened to our community.

We innately knew something was wrong because we were displaced. We moved from our block to a project at 129th Street between Seventh and Eight Avenues. The St. Nicholas Projects.

Being teenagers we walked into high school from a Catholic school where everybody had smocks to niggas wearing cordovans while we had holes in our shoes. We had to fight because guys would always give us those funny looks.

I think we lost a lot of desire to go to school then and we would spend more time singing. We formed a little group and instead of going to school we would spend time drinking and singing doowop. There was a basic moral breakdown that started when we left the block, went to the projects, and started going to public schools.

High school was our true introduction to drugs and alcohol. Which was totally OK with us.

We were coming out of a private school where we sat in one class all day with one teacher who knew everything about us and even knew us apart. To go to a class where they didn't even know you were a twin—that was fun. Like, "Hey Arthur, you got this class and I'll go to the bathroom."

We had a total breakdown. It was like breakdown city. Our parents couldn't recognize the breakdown because our father had already broken down. They were also the first generation in the city so they had no references on what to expect or know what reefer was. And we took full advantage of all of that.

One of our saving graces was we maintained our musical ambitions—and we had a mentor named Ironhead. We called him Ironhead because he was a weightlifter, and he always taught us about how to eat to live and how to train. He used to tell us things like, "Do everything in moderation," when he saw us going a little overboard. But he gave us a foundation to run back to. How to clean your system and regenerate.

He always said he was God, which we thought was blasphemous, because we were Christians. But we liked him anyway. He had a magnificent physique and we always said, "This is the kind of body we want," so we could endure him being blasphemous.

We started with him around the age of eight, and we stayed with him until his death last year at 104.

He used to say that no matter where we got to in life, he'd be ahead of us.

We said, "What about when you die?"

He said, "I'll be ahead of you there too."

He told us that man was God, that all of this religious bullshit was bullshit, and we waited for the lightning bolt to come down and hit him. When it didn't, we started studying a little harder.

He was one of the most incredible men you could have ever met. A Harlem legend known by many people. If we ever get into the position, we would love to have a statue built of him.

But to get back to the breakdown: high school for us was literally that, because we stayed high. We perfected our singing craft, but nothing else.

We often have nightmares to this day of trying to find our way to a class.

We would often sneak out and see the Dean of Discipline and he would be happy we were out of school, this Dean of Discipline. It was a conspiracy.

Our next move after high school was to look for our economic program.

Taharqa: At this point I went to the army. I'm seventeen years old, it's 1964, and I was very disenchanted and frustrated with everything—with my parents, with living at home.

Tundera: I didn't go in because I was shot during the Harlem riots. I used to be patriotic and would get upset that he didn't want to wear his uniform when he came home on leave.

Taharqa: Part of that was based on my attitude. I brought into the army a New York attitude. I noticed that New Yorkers were profiled in the military. As a young New Yorker you might as well have been a hiphopper. Couldn't nobody tell you nothing. The military's purpose was to indoctrinate you, but I had my new doctrine which I had learned in high school. "Nigga-anity" was my new religion, and the military obviously didn't like it.

I did learn a lot about comradery in the army, though. I had friends and lost a lot of people there when we were sent to Vietnam. I learned a lot about another way of love and brotherhood even though I was slow to learn. (I objected to learning anything new because I was still bathing and basking in my new religion of Nigga-anity.) When they declared war on Vietnam they lied to us and told us we were going over there to be advisers. We had no skills for a jungle war. When they told us what to expect, they said, "Marijuana, partying, and freaky young Oriental women." That's what they lured the seventeen-year-olds over there with.

Tundera: While he was doing that, I was receiving my indoctrination in the streets. I was in a singing group that was really, really good called the GTOs, named after the car. Someone told us there was a Black record company in Harlem.

When we went over there we noticed there were all kinds of Cadillacs and Electra 225s parked in front, all the latest cars. Sharp-looking young guys were going into this record shop and we found out that it was a drug-dealing spot—one of the biggest in Harlem. We thought were going in for an audition but when we got in there we saw all these guys our age in alligator shoes and really looking sharp.

They weren't paying too much attention to us, but the main character was—a big Black cat who looked like Idi Amin. He was dressed impeccably and he jumped out of this big limousine and listened to our audition. He looked suspicious, but we thought, What the hell, he owns a record company, hey, that's good enough for us. In the middle of the audition, though, he fell asleep, and we come to find out he had diabetes.

There was something about us that attracted his attention. We were all young, good-looking guys, we had our music together, and he decided to let us into his fold.

When we got into the fold we found out that the record company was nothing but a front, and that he was a drug czar. But that was OK because I knew I had to have some kind of way of supporting myself.

Taharqa: I noticed something was changing when he wrote me letters.

Tundera: I probably had a little more cockiness because now I had some money.

Taharqa: I remember I came back from the Army on leave and told him he needed to watch his back or something was going to happen.

Tundera: He left and four days later the Harlem riots happened and I got shot in the back. After that, though, I became the drug czar's lieutenant, and wound up making all sorts of money. I used to write Taharqa and tell him, "Come home, we have arrived." At that time I had two cars, a home, and an apartment.

There was a whole crew of us that started a concept called "Harlem World" that later on became an actual club and one of the birthplaces of hiphop. Under this "Harlem World" concept our plan was to take control of Harlem.

What happened was we wound up having different spots. Like broaster chicken houses, because they were popular in Philly (and anything that was popular in Philly we tried to emulate). We also had chitlin houses, conch houses, steak houses—anything we thought would fly. It never really worked because nobody knew how to work a business. Everybody was really hustlers and would go into the cash register and take the money.

But now most of the musicians when they came to New York would frequent our establishments, because we had fantastic girls and fantastic parties.

There was also a record label named after the two main drug guys.

The beauty of the main guy was that though he was a very powerful figure in Harlem, many people didn't know he was gay also. He had this persona of this awful gangster but one of his fetishes was young boys. He would set up these lavish parties so that everybody could just freak together. Weird things used to occur around these parties.

We had a huge apartment over on Riverside that had a bar with everything. Like we had a table full of pure cocaine. It was like *Superfly* for real.

One day we were waiting for this guy to come from Chicago or Detroit and buy a kilo. Our plan was to make the deal, sell the coke, and then have a party.

The guy came in. Immaculate, young dude, couldn't have been more than twenty-three. He went over, sniffed the cocaine, and dropped dead.

It was surreal.

Everybody was already high, completely zonked, been tootin' all day. He comes in, takes his little blow, and drops dead.

Now the party was the important thing. The money and the party were the most important things on our minds. Him dropping dead is like a damper on the whole thing.

Or—and this is the point—it could have been a damper. But nothing is necessarily a damper because everything can move on if you're creative enough.

Everybody is sitting there in a stupor, trying to figure out what to do. Then one brilliant high mind comes up with a creative idea: Let's take him, put him in the basement, and let the fun begin. So they moved the body into the basement and proceeded to have their fun.

I'll never forget how even in my stupor I thought, There's something wrong with this, but what the hell—too many fine girls up in here.

These parties became so well known that they became frequented by some of the top Black entertainers of the day. So whoever came to the Apollo would become a part of our Harlem World situation.

Now through all of that the music was prevalent. It took a secondary position to the drugs and the money, but we were meeting some of the top people in the industry. And we would say to the main guy, "What about us going into the studio?" So even in our stupor we would try to pull things together and make the music happen.

Like let's say a Bobby Womack comes through. The main guy might say, "Hey, Bobby, write a song for my group."

So Bobby would say, "OK." And he'd start doing a song he had on the shelf somewhere that Sam Cooke or somebody didn't do, a reject. The group would start working on it on the spot.

This scene was also a breeding ground for young musicians and producers—Blowfly, the GQs, LTD, Big Maybelle, Sam and Dave—everybody was there so it was a musical family as well.

So in spite of everything that was going on we were still trying to achieve our ultimate goal of a Harlem World recording studio and a serious independent Black record and distribution company. Berry Gordy had shown us that it could be done.

The main guy had created this other atmosphere where we could learn about the music industry. He had records and we learned about production and distribution.

There was also an organization called the Fair Play Committee that was about making radio accountable to the community. It was a very conducive time for Black people to take advantage of their opportunities in music.

There was a young lady who was part of our scene at the time. She used to tell me about these two guys. One was allegedly the father of her child—a Harlem gangster. The other was this cute guy, she claimed, named Jimmy, who was a musician that played with all the groups around. All the girls, she said, really liked him, and she thought I should meet him because I'd really like him.

Now my ego was such that I didn't really want to meet no other nigga, because by now I think I'm Big Daddy. I thought I had arrived. So another guy? And a pseudo musician at that? Because I'm thinking I know all the real musicians, like James Brown. So don't tell me about some guitarist you in love with when I love you, baby.

But she also told me this Jimmy was staying with this fine little girl she wanted me to meet. My friend was a networker and I think she wanted me to pimp this girl. I think she had an ulterior motive, which was to get Jimi out of that girl's house, which was at Parkwest Village over on 100th Street and Eighth Avenue.

When my friend took me up to the girl's place, Jimi wasn't there. Me and the girl clicked immediately, just like my friend had predicted. Obviously she had been telling the girl about me so it was like a match made in heaven. Overnight we became lovers and Jimi wasn't even an issue.

We were chillin' when one day out of the blue, the doorbell rings and it's Jimi. He wasn't *Jimi Hendrix*, but he walks in and assesses the situation and sees that obviously I was the new guy who had replaced him.

Immediately all he wanted to know was, "Are my records still there? Didja throw my shit out?"

But my friend introduced us and I got a good feeling from him. He didn't look physically threatening at all. Nor did it look as though he could take over my position as the head of the house. I felt no threat from him whatsoever so it was OK that he stayed. And my friend had also told me so much about him that I was looking forward to meeting him.

Jimi had a room in the apartment and that was OK with me. It wasn't OK with the girl. She wanted him out of there and my job was to get Jimi Hendrix the fuck out of the house.

"Too many memories," and "Now your job, nigga, as my pimp, is to get rid of him." Like, "That's why I got you. To get rid of him."

But I began to like him.

He would come in almost like a mouse that didn't want to breathe no air. Didn't want to eat your food or anything. He would just come in humble.

Of course when I saw that he always had his guitar, I got guilty. Because by this time I'm hustling real hard but his attitude about music and his discipline took me back to my sister. Through him I'm seeing what it takes to become really successful in music. I'm seeing him listening to these records constantly and going over licks and these little things and listening to blues and going to the roots of music. This at a time when I associated the blues with the guy who got his ear cut off with a bottle.

Little by little my music started to come out of me. And little by little I'm really beginning to like this guy because he's showing me something. He was more like an angel than an adversary or a threat. I really believe he was there to put things back in perspective for me because I was beginning to lose consciousness and all sight of priorities.

Meanwhile the girl was pressuring me to throw him out. We had a big argument and I told her as long as I was here, he could stay.

He was there for maybe a couple of weeks just hanging around but he didn't just hang—he was studying. He wasn't asking for no pussy or no money. He was like a monk.

Taharqa: When I came home from the Army in 1966 and saw this guy sitting on the floor with his guitar it didn't mathematically compute to me either. I'm like, "Who is he?"

But then I felt the same thing Tunde felt, which is that, wow, this is what it's truly all about. You could barely hear the strings but you knew that that this guy was serious.

He didn't say much because he never knew how we might come at him. He was always conscious of the fact that we could be savages, that we could be beasts. Because we were attempting to take on the gangster demeanor, he didn't know that music was truly our roots. We dressed like the street, with the rings and things. And with me just coming home from the military, jumping into his way of life, I'm also coming home with a killer's mindset from Vietnam. I'm desensitized, so show me a life to take. When I came home Jimi might have been a perfect candidate for elimination.

But like Tunde said, he evoked in me a sense of our roots and our sister Alma, who we had the utmost reverence for. It was almost like we heard our mother saying, "Flank up, take your position, boys." And I think Jimi began to sense that we took our positions and were very protective of him. He became a symbol of our sister to us and, no matter how intimidating we were, I think he felt more comfortable and protected around us because it was this spiritual thing.

Tundera: I also didn't know until he came back from England that he had heard the argument between me and the girl about him.

What happened was that he disappeared as mysteriously as he had come.

Faye [Pridgeon, Jimi's ex-girlfriend] told us how he was playing around with Little Richard and how the girls loved him, but it wasn't James Brown and we didn't want to hear that shit. Our allegiance wasn't about him as a sexy guitarist or whatever he was grooming himself to be. We went beyond that to the fact that through him, we were protecting music and trying to manage our own guilt. We knew that in order to become successful in music we had to discipline ourselves on his level. We had touched that level, through our sister, so we had respect for it.

But when he left it was no big thing. It actually made my job easier because there was no more pressure from the girl.

In my heart, though, I always wondered whatever happened to that nigga. He was gone and he stayed away for almost two years.

Then one day, all of sudden, I called my mother's house and she said, "Come over to the house. Faye is here and there's a surprise."

When I got there Faye and Jimi were sitting down but it wasn't the same guy. The humility was there but there was more confidence. He was like a fully evolved young god and he wasn't afraid to breathe your air anymore.

When he saw me he lit up like a Christmas tree.

Because remember, in my mother's house the piano was there, and there were pictures, and there was a feeling of music emanating from the place because my mother and my sister were musicians. When he walked in the house he probably felt more warm about us than ever before.

And with Faye always championing us, Jimi probably had a good picture of who we really were. He looked at me as though he was able to see that. And from that day forth, almost a whole other world opened up.

It was almost like Jimi became obsessed with getting us out of Harlem and bringing us into the new world. He would create situations for us, create scenarios for us, create relationships for us. That goes on to this day.

(Whenever we're financially low, the song "Freedom" will play on a commercial and we always get checks from it. For the past twenty-five years we've been reaping the rewards of our relationship with Jimi and he never lets us down. We never need money because he always makes sure that something comes through for us.) Now when he came to my mother's house with Faye he had the first Experience album. And when Jimi presented it to us we were very elated.

We hadn't followed his career other than hearing Faye say, "Oh, Jimi is doing good in Europe." When he presented us with the album we didn't realize his magnitude or that he was getting ready to break here. We took it as though he was a new artist that had broke Over There somewhere. (*Where* we didn't know. Overseas to Black people at that time was very vague.)

So he gave us a copy of that album. A very different look, but it was Jimi, so we held onto that. We took it home. Now remember, this is during that very serious Motown, James Brown, Sly Stone, time. That was the musical order of the day that we were programmed to respond to. And because we're around music all the time, trying to get our little group together, we have what we think is a concept of what music is supposed to be. We're building this label and we think we've got Knowledge.

So we ran home and put the record on the turntable and we were like, "Where's the single?" I think we became the first breakbeat deejays skipping through the record looking for the single.

We were extremely disappointed but frightened for Jimi. How could we go back and tell him, "This shit ain't happening"? We thought, Poor Jimi, he got his hopes up high for this shit?

So now for the first time in our lives we're challenged. We can't go back and tell this boy his record is garbage. There's got to be one single on there.

We know how hard this boy worked when he was in our house. We thought, It's going to be back to the ghetto because this was not going to work in America. So we had to find one that might work in America. Let's roll up our sleeves and work hard to find one single because we might have to take this to Frankie Crocker for our man. We have to find something Frankie would like. Because Frankie came through our parties and we took it as our responsibility to look out for Jimi. He put it in our hands, so maybe he needs our help. That's our own ego, I guess. We have to fix the whole world.

I'll never forget: I was living in a nice high-rise on Ninth Avenue and 19th Street. We were going over and over and over Jimi's album.

Now remember, we're brainwashed. And when you first threw Hendrix on back then, it was like, walk, don't run out of the door quick. It's like, what the fuck is going on here?

We had to love him to even listen because our thinking is really not even *Afro* but *processed*.

But what happened was the ballads made us calm down. Even though Jimi's ballads weren't traditional, it was something we could listen to.

And as we started listening to them, it made us realize, hey there's a production going on here. Something serious is happening.

All that "Purple Haze" was almost sacrilegious to us.

"Red House" was on there, but what we knew about the blues came from living on 141st St. where most of the people who liked the blues was winos and alcoholics. Like the guy who got his ear knocked off.

There was a guy in the neighborhood whose face was all cut up, his name was Cabbage—every night he listened to the blues. So the blues? Oh no, no, no, not the blues.

"Wind Cries Mary" was what we could identify with.

I'll never forget that day. I'll never forget the magic started to come over us. Like a veil came from over our eyes. I'll never forget that day.

It was like we realized this guy was different, and where different usually meant something was bad, this guy was different with something going for himself.

This was some really special shit we're listening to. And it made us listen even deeper.

So it started with love to even listen to the feedback and the sounds we couldn't even get with at the time.

From love for Jimi it moved to respect and then to love for the music.

And I think from that revelation it became easier for us to even deal with that life energy that he began to represent in his dress. Because he was in Harlem not only bringing this new sound, but he was wearing bell-bottoms and bringing this new look as well. Even the car he chose, a little Corvette, was new, when the style of the day was Cadillacs and Electra 225s.

It was like, Man, can't but two people get in that, you are way out there. But allowances were made because we were looking for something new.

And in a strange way he came and offered us a way out, because Harlem was getting boring to us. When Jimi would come in and jam at Small's Paradise with King Curtis, Lonnie Youngblood, or Jimmy Castor—people who maintained a high standard of musicianship—he would lift the place up to another level. He raised the standard and everybody was aware of it.

The musicians in Harlem knew Jimi very well from the circuit but not the level of his success—but they would always let him play.

There was only one person I recall who said, "No, *emphatically,* no," and embarrassed the three of us and made us leave the club with our heads hung low.

Because when Jimi would go in and play he would totally take control. His whole objective was to destroy.

We didn't realize that and he used us to get into a lot of places.

He set niggas up. So that instead of people loving the artist who was there they wound up loving Jimi.

But the one person who was very aware of that was Richie Havens. Richie Havens wasn't having it.

"Can I play, Richie?"

"No." And emphatic. Like, you ain't fucking with me. Your reputation precedes you, boy. Get outta here. He was the only one I know who was smart enough to stop Hendrix from coming up.

Some people think the energy that made Hendrix came from the guitar or from the writing, but it was none of that. From our perspective, studying the situation over the years and being able to verbalize it, you're dealing with an entity or energy that was beyond just a guitar or a lyricist or a person that was a famous entertainer.

Somebody once asked Jimi, "What would you do if you weren't playing guitar?"

He said, "Anything I do, I would put that same passion into it, and I would be great at whatever I did." It blew our minds when he said that.

Because if he was just sweeping the floor he would have been the greatest floor sweeper in the world. It would have been a revolutionary thing in floor sweeping. Like, no man has ever swept a floor this way. Look upon it.

When he was playing there were certain energies around him and he was clearly communicating with those energies.

I often wondered, Did his power come from these energies? Did they come from him or from outside of him? Were they hanging out with him? Did they talk to him? Did they say, Hey Jimi, we chose you and we're going to give you whatever we have to give —the magic we have for you to be such and such.

He wanted us to see that there was something beyond what you normally see around him. He wanted us to see that here was a whole other reality, that he communicated with these entities or energies, they communicated with him, and they were like music itself.

Did these energies like him? Was there a love affair going on with these music entities and him? Did they say, Hey we're going to give you all the powers you need and when people see you they're going to feel this type of energy? Everybody won't see us, but people will feel the magnetic glow coming from you. Did he make a deal with them?

Sometimes when we listen to Stevie Wonder's music we say, "This man made a deal with somebody."

When you look at music, you say, dig: if music has a life-intelligence (and we know that it has an intelligence), when you look at the spirit of music, it seems that for various reasons there are people it wants to give itself to and lend itself to. Maybe because of the discipline of that individual, maybe because of what it wants out of that individual. And sometimes, when the individual can't totally give music what it wants, it may just, like a drug, or anything else, be done with the host. And look for someone who might be even more amenable.

I think that music experiments with people, and if they can't give music what it truly wants . . . because it's looking at people like Miles and John Coltrane and Jimi and Charlie Parker. Very intense powerful people who might have fucked up with what they were hosting, and not understood what they were supposed to do.

I'm sure music used Jimi.

You know, it's funny, but Taharqa and I often discuss those pictures Monika Danneman took of Jimi at the very end of Jimi's life. There are some of those pictures where I don't see that energy around him anymore.

That same energy that I remember from when that young boy walked into that girl's house and kept me at bay from kicking him out.

The same energy we saw when he left to go to the Isle of Wight and the two of us sat in a car on 59th while he sat on the curb. (And we had a long discussion—a whole meeting—right on the street about what we were going to do next.)

We talked to Jimi when he was on the Isle of Wight. And in every picture we could see him exuberant, illuminating that energy, somewhat concealed but still revealing itself.

But in some of those pictures we saw at the very end it was absent.

It was almost as though that energy knew this host wasn't going to hold on any longer. The energies said, I'm outta here. And they left first.

Ronnie Drayton

Courtesy Ronnie Drayton

One of the first articles I wrote after moving from Washington, D.C., to New York in 1982 was on Ronnie Drayton. I had seen him playing at D.C.'s 9:30 club with Deadline, an instrumental power trio featuring Drayton and drummer Phillip Wilson and led by Bill Laswell. I was immediately struck by his harmonically rich rhythm concept and, most of all, his tone. It worked from that space in between distorted and clean, metal and country. It was a tone quality also favored by Hendrix and, later, Eddie Van Halen, who would define his version as "the brown sound." When I caught up with Drayton in New York a few years later, he was routinely performing with James Blood Ulmer, Nona Hendryx, and jazz vibraphonist Jay Hoggard.

Turns out I had actually heard Drayton's playing long before I knew his name, because he had appeared on a Black Rock classic, Edwin Birdsong's Supernatural, released in 1972. As I got to know him, I discovered he had worked with a host of people in rock, jazz, fusion, and rhythm and blues—the Chambers Brothers, Wilson Pickett, Roy Ayers, Ryuichi Sakamoto, and David Sylvain among them.

In many ways his path had been a mirror-image of Hendrix's before Jimi's transatlantic sojourn. The consummate sideman who transcended the description with unique chordal voicings, lefthanded inversions that favored the low end, and punctuated rhythm in ways that swung harder than your average bassist or drummer.

Drayton is also a phenomenally moving soloist who credits Albert King with embarrassing him into trying to squeeze as much emotional content as possible from a single note. "Albert was backstage once and he said, 'All you New York guitar players with your thousand notes.' He played one note that made all the beer in the room go flat."

As a performer Drayton has a way of synchronizing his body with his sonic escapades that resembles Hendrix. He is also as thoughtful, idiosyncratic, and incisive a commentator on guitar technique and guitar strategy as you're likely to find this side of Robert Fripp.

How did Jimi affect me? That's a deep one.

I played drums before guitar. As a teenager I was one of the better drummers in Queens.

Omar Hakim and Marcus Miller were just kids then. But around 1967, there was a guitar player named Robert Rudolph who was, of all things, a Jehovah's Witness. He was very lanky like Jimi and he was imitating Jimi to no end. He was always the guitarist in these rhythm and blues bands I was hitting with, and he was the one who officially turned me on to the sound of James Marshall Hendrix.

I kept telling him I was going to meet Hendrix one day.

He just laughed and said, "Everybody says that."

My mom was a classical pianist and a prima ballerina. My uncle was a woodwind player who hung out with Harry Belafonte. They used to go see Trane and everybody from that whole era of the '50s.

We were living in Manhattan on Adam Clayton Powell Boulevard and then later we moved to Brooklyn.

My mom and my uncle were Catholic school kids out rebelling. The hip thing with Black people at that time was, Put your kids in a good school. The best school was a Catholic school. (They couldn't get us into the Yeshivas. That was very rare.)

They started directing me to music in Catholic school in the second or third grade when I was maybe eight or nine. But the first recollection of me being able to hum a song was at four. (I was talking fluently at two, they tell me, and trying to run things and getting my ass kicked).

I taught myself how to play drums at eight or nine in elementary school.

I didn't pick up the guitar until I was about 17 or 18 years old after this Robert Randolph guy played me the *Are You Experienced* record. I played drums with him in this band called the Soul Shakers with Mic Murphy who was in the System later on—he had a Country Gentlemen guitar I used to freak out on because it had a whammy bar. I was always twiddling with that guitar and they got mad at me because I was starting to play the guitar better than the guitar player in the band.

From that contact with Robert and another guitar player named Robert Fontaine and these other cats who were Christian Scientists in this six-month period. . . . (This is a deep story because all these people were from these wild religious backgrounds: Fontaine was a Baptist. The other crew who taught me my first three chords were Seventh Day Adventists so there was this weird synergy you know? All these people who were being called outcast for listening to this devil music by this skinny, light-skinned devil making these voodoo tones.)

In any event, I got a guitar and I spent one year just staying in the basement, listening to the radio. Got a couple of Mel Bay books and by osmosis, in a year's time, I could play whole songs off the hit list without even thinking about it.

Being an only child, Jimi came through for me as my way out of Queens and the whole emotional only-child turmoil of a father-done-bounced and my mother . . . God rest her soul, she died in a mental institution. Not a lot of people know this. My grandmother did the best she could. My uncle was a freakin' gangster who worked for Nicky Barnes's numbers-running and dope operation in Harlem. So already I'm set up in a position to be a spoiled only-child megalomaniac gangster or just out of here. My one saving grace before I discovered Jimi was I loved playing the drums.

The rhythm thing I just picked up. I can remember walking past this church in Brooklyn on Bedford and Nostrand with my uncle and hearing these drums. I said, "Uncle Rudolph, I can play these drums."

Next thing I know my uncle was saying, "Boy, you can't play no drums."

But then this gangster with his Al Packards and his snakeskin shoes, looking like Mister Pimpman, Mister Drug Man, he said, "If you can play the drums, I'll buy you a set of drums."

And I said, "Oh really?" Because I knew he had crazy paper on him all the time.

Well, I got in that church, got on them drums, turned that beat around, and I played there all day long. And my Uncle Rudolph sat there. Probably the longest time he'd been in a church in a long time. And he got me my first set of drums.

Jimi became a preoccupation for me not only because of how his soloing grabbed me, but because I played drums, and understood how the drums worked in the rhythm section. So the whole relationship he had with Mitch Mitchell was messing me up. Because I knew from playing in an ensemble how one thing plays off another, and when I was listening to his stuff, I thought, How is he doing this? I knew there was something he was doing that I had to learn how to do from the feeling the music was giving me and because he was way the hell ahead of me. This rhythm thing he had going on was unnerving to me.

Back then we had the turntables with the 33 1/3 and 16 rpms and I used to slow Jimi's records down to figure out his intentions.

The first thing old players told me was always try to figure out a player's intent. Find out why is he playing *this* in his eight bars. Transcribe the parts and figure out what they're saying. What is their story?

I couldn't read music then. All I had was ears and a killer stereo. But I'm listening to how this guy constructed these guitar parts and I'm listening to his sound and his sense of orchestration and, always, the rhythm, the rhythm, the rhythm. The way these guitar parts were singing against each other. I used to call it "singing" until one day in church, this lady said to me, "When you hear these people singing they're singing contrapuntally—calling and answering one another's part." This is what James does when he is playing against himself so well. When you think about one person subdividing himself that way, it boggles the mind.

Hearing him led me to deeper into voicings and chords and playing upside down and moving chords around in a way other guys don't.

It was natural for me to play left-handed like him because going to Catholic school they wanted me to write right-handed. And my grandmother was like, "Next time you come at my grandson with some nonsense, Sister Marie, I'm going to kick your ass, or have my daughter kick your ass." The next time they did something to me in school, I was taken out of the class and my mother literally beat this lady up in the classroom for trying to make us write right-handed. (My mom was left-handed. Florence Drayton, she was a genius. The space she was in life was not a good space for her to express all of that. But all my analytical ability comes from her. Because her analytical perception was way ahead of its time. She was a genius, really, which made it difficult to comprehend her sometimes.)

What also got to me was what a pure tone James had, chordally, and in a solo context.

My uncle had gotten me listening to so many horns, from Coltrane to Rufus Harley on bagpipes to Cannonball Adderley to every flautist around. So I had woodwinds in my head all the time just blowing these screeching tones.

Then I heard Jimi playing in this electric environment with a control over his tone like a horn player's. Only deeper than that—he took an idiom like the blues, with all that pain, and was able to fill that space with a tone that was so pure. To this day, it's his use of his tone and the way his pain flowed out of his body through that tone that gets me.

He found a vehicle that pulls young people to him as an artist. Because what he's doing is tapping into our pain, our feeling of being abandoned or whatever we were going through as children. The only thing that's like that today is hiphop because of the angst in it.

When I was learning guitar my grandmother used to say, "Why are you playing these blues? I've had enough blues. I've seen men hung in the streets. You better learn some of this happy music."

But she understood when I said, "I've got to learn how to do this."

His tone, his use of space, and there's the killer: his respect for space in his phrasing combined with his tone. It was never about ego or about having to control another player.

When you hear him jamming with other players he's always supportive and always gives the other player plenty of space before he comes back and blows them out.

What he's doing is defining the space through his use of space, like Miles did. If you listen to what's going on in the pauses of his music—like in

"Machine Gun," after you hear him sing "So let your bullets fly down like rain," you hear him take a breath before that first solo, and when that tone hits, it's coming from a pure rhythm and blues space, a pure Zeppelin space (which was really his rhythm in the pure sense).

That's the thing that puzzled me so much about him as a soloist and a composer because his sensibilities were so orchestral. They're majestic. And with just a six-string guitar, a wah-wah pedal, and in the studio spinning the tape machine backward. These were the limited tools he used to create these sonic environments that are so poignant.

He makes you listen, this guy. And I give him mad love for this: he makes you get educated. You listen to James and you get educated.

Just like Charlie Parker did, and he was doing it sick on dope. Trying to get the next hit, being so ill he probably didn't want to waste time getting to the next bar line so he just flew through 'em.

Jimi, on other hand, had people in there playing with him twenty-four hours a day.

Now I got this Johnny Cochran sidebar: James Marshall Hendrix was not a dope addict. That just makes me angry when I hear people still say that to this day. He experimented like a lot of us did, but he was no dope fiend.

What Jimi did that the jazz guys didn't was that he took the pain of incarceration and slavery in the cotton fields, and people shouting at the top of their lungs about oppression in rhythm and hoping to get out of this oppression. He took all that and he brought it through the rhythm and blues music of the day, which was very technical music, and he created a very pure fusion, much like the way the great bop players did moving all those scales, Lydian to chromatic, around so it was one fluid language.

But Jimi took blues, rhythm and blues, and jazz elements and created a completely fluid fusion that also involved his speaking voice, which he used as another instrument, another rhythm. Bob Dylan gave him that concept, which was brilliant.

But he took the pain of the blues and put it back in pop music and put it back in people's faces. He put Albert King and B. B. King and Muddy Waters in people's faces the way the jazz guys didn't. When he bent his notes you heard all of that.

Back then, guys did not bend notes with the accuracy James did. They would always have that shrill vibrato or too much vibrato. Or they'd bend a note a semitone above or a semitone below; but every time James would bend a note it would be like Albert or B.B. Every time they bent a note their pitch was spot on, every single time. (Albert only has eight notes but he flips them around so many different ways.)

James is the most vocal guitarist ever because he plays as he sings. James's tone doesn't sound like it comes from his fingers. His vibrato is like a singer moving through his head voice and his chest voice.

I know they say a guitar player's tone comes from his hands, and it is true. But when you listen to him you can hear the subtlety of how he moves the string across the fret. With most guitar players you hear them think before they move their hands. With James it just goes and it flows.

He was around all these great singers and all these great bands, like Ike Turner's. Ike was a killer with his rhythm concept too. Ike's band, Joe Tex's band, the Isley Brothers and Dyke and the Blazers and Sam Cooke's band, all those bands were tight, mechanized units that Jimi learned from. He took all that stuff and he figured out how he could use his tone inside of those structures and as a way to express his pain.

All this stuff is very entwined.

Jimi was raised in poverty. His grandmother was a full-blooded Cherokee. One thing people don't acknowledge about Hendrix is the real essence of his playing, which is his pain from being rejected and being abandoned by his mother.

As a single parent of a teenage male I understand Jimi's dad more than ever. His having to create the stability of two parents for a child.

Jimi couldn't just come out and acknowledge his roots. There was so much pain he was trying to deal with and he was just trying to figure out ways to say these things.

With any human being, though, after so many years of being bombarded with information, when the portal opens for you to really express things, all that information and all that pain just comes out. Like when you hear that song "Gypsy Eyes," there's the Cherokee in that rhythm right there. My grandmother heard that and said, "That boy sounds like an Indian. Is he an Indian?" She used to say, "That boy got pain. He plays like an old man. That's an old soul. He won't be here too long. That weight he's carrying is too heavy." I never understood what she meant by that until much later on.

When you've got to express all of that pain your internals are doing a search to find something to tap off of, you get a sound and a feeling and then, Bang!

I think at the time that he died, Jimi was about to tap into stuff we don't have any inkling about. Because James Marshall Hendrix was a very smart guy. Look at his career: a perfect setup.

With *Are You Experienced*: it's experimental, brand-new, a perfect fusion of pop, rock and roll, and funk.

Axis: Bold As Love is the next step after that. Again, perfect timing: people are getting high, having sex all the time, the culture is still about freedom.

Then he takes it another notch up with *Electric Ladyland,* which is using new technology to get the message across and the messages he's throwing about life—whew! This is the pinnacle and he's creating it while flying all over the world, doing two hundred dates a year.

Now we roll up to *Band of Gypsys,* and *Band of Gypsys* is for Black people to understand where his funk was coming from. His management circle kept Black people filtered from him, but when he understood that, he drops the record that becomes the setup for all the Black rock and roll bands and the heavy metal of the day.

Now people tried to say that *Band of Gypsys* setup was plodding and that it was this and it was that, but Zeppelin was trying to plod the same way and Black Sabbath trying to plod even harder than that. *Band of Gypsys* was the real divining rod in terms of finding this new water to drink from, and everybody was trying to drink from it, bro'. I was drinking, and when P-funk came around there was not one guitar player who was not playing some of that stuff. Some of that energy even infused their rhythm sections. The Hendrix element is a definitive reference with the P-funk crew and the way their guitars swing and the way Bernie Worrel's clavinet swings, and Bootsy is just pure Jimi.

I can take songs apart and tell you where bands have taken if not the same licks and the same phrases, then the same feelings, per se, of *Band of Gypsys.* The way the rhythm resolves on the one all the time. That thing that comes from Africa through James Brown and Jimi. That's pure African and pure American Indian too. Because American Indians have that thing where they play back against the beat or on the and-the-one, just like you hear in the church. It's just naturally the way we walk whether I'm walking in Queens or you're walking in Brooklyn or Kansas City or Seattle. If there's a concentration of us in a space, this is how we're going to feed ourselves, is with that rhythm.

Another thing with us is how we take our pain and then shift it into positivity, and that really depends on our swing also. I'm not a negative person who talks about music being better yesterday. We've always had our pop icons and our bullshit records. But if we're talking about consciously elevating people, none of this music today is doing that like Jimi did.

I don't think he thought he was doing anything deep. He was just trying to play what was on his head, but it's taken us years to catch up. I mean he's been dead how many years and it's like he's still here walking down the block when you look at style, culture, ways of speaking, and songs. Like "Freedom" showing up on Toyota commercials and whatnot.

The thing with Jimi is, on the one hand, he wanted to be in a position to make sure he could eat and survive better. But on the other hand he probably had symphonic technicolor dreams like Mozart.

That's not that unusual. But it's the people who can pull it together to create a synergy with the rest of us that are rare. And when he finally got in an environment where he could create, the Lord put everything in order for him.

Because he walked in the studio and there was Eddie Kramer who had just come from working with George Martin and the Beatles. Eddie was like a razor who respected that Jimi was a more complete guitarist than anybody in England at the time, more than Beck, or Clapton, or any of them. And when Jimi started talking about what he was hearing in sonic terms, Eddie understood what he meant. Like when Jimi got to talking about guitars being flipped left and right, Eddie understood that meant panning. And when he said, "I hear the guitars spinning backward," Eddie was like, "All right, we'll splice the tape, flip it over," and we got that sound he had learned to produce working on those Beatles productions. Eddie understood about EQ and about presence.

So now Jimi can take all those things he sees in his dreams or sees when he's having a joint or when he's about to have an orgasm, or all those parts he hears when he's just playing the guitar by himself. Now he's got a way to catalog it, and he's going nuts. When they gave him the overdub that was it. The cat's out of the bag.

You've got to give Eddie Kramer credit. Eddie Kramer is a bad man in terms of how he was able to connect with someone and bring all of those ideas to life. He did that and there's no doubt about it.

The way those records are EQ'd and those guitars were miked—people think it's all these big amplifiers going but it was just Fender Twins and tweets and slanted Marshalls with ten-inch speakers. And for him to be able to play that loud and get the tones they were getting tells you something about the microphones they were using and the cables from the microphones to the pre-amp to those old desks. All that stuff you don't hear now and that maybe you're not supposed to hear.

Just like great writers find a way to get you inside their books and make you travel with them, a few guitar players can make you travel with them inside of their sounds and their pedals. James, Jeff Beck, Adrian Belew. Steve Vai, who has his moments. They all have this way of getting inside of a pedal and extracting some magic from it because they've found out that they live there. They live inside of this tonally dense, thin-atmosphere environment where they can turn the lights on in the building at will. That's a gift: to get it all to work together as one complete flow. It becomes a place where now all their ideas get tied together.

Like Jimi knew that if I have my Marshall amp turned at this angle and I stand at this angle three or four feet away, or whatever, and I hit this chord, I know I'm going to get this response. And I know if I hit this note at this place on the neck with just a little bit of overdrive, or if I use this little bit of Fuzzface or wah-wah like a preamp to throw more gain into the line, then I can control the feedback like a violin or like a saxophone.

If you watch him, you see him breathing when he's playing like a horn player doing circular breathing. So you hear that long breath like a stream-of-consciousness as he finds a way to get into the pedal and tweak the thing to his personal frequency so he can tune into that frequency at will.

That's how guys get into a pedal. That's why guys disappear and don't talk to their girlfriends for days, weeks, months, and stay in there with that gear to figure out how to get that sound. I still do it.

For most of us, it's never perfected, but James had it down. And because now we're talking about a personality as big as that building across the street, when we give him a pedal he can tweak, oh my goodness! It's like giving him a freaking bazooka, dogg. Combine that with his control over his tone, and that tone is pure Stratocaster—look out, yo.

People didn't know what a Stratocaster was until James took it and said, "This is what you do with a Stratocaster." I think he was drawn to it because of the tonal versatility of the guitar. Three pickups, two tone controls, and the volume. The pickup selector switch is such that if you flick it and put it in the middle by accident you go out-of-phase and that creates these tones that the old school rhythm and blues players knew all about.

What happened with James, though, was he learned that when you turned the guitar up louder it became more of a vocal instrument. The Strat simply has more of a vocal sound than, say, a Les Paul. People say it sounded thinner because it didn't have the humbucker pickups of a Les Paul but they didn't know how to EQ it. James knew how to EQ it.

Xenobia Bailey

Photo by Ron Monk

This woman performs miracles with yarn, crochet hook, and needles—multicolored, multitextured, life-size miracles. Her art is composed of yarn, and every composition tells a story. She has built life-size juju figures out of yarn; crocheted ten-foot-tall tents out of four-ply yarn big enough for your average nuclear family to sit in; stitched cosmic tapestry mandalas, including one in human form that can hypnotize you on sight.

Xenobia hails from roughly the same time and the same community in Seattle as Hendrix, and can recall him as an older kid who came by her house a few times to hang out on the block of 26th and E. Helen with his cool-natured but fiery younger brother Leon. Jimi would eventually sit down on the corner curve and watch one of his dream girls lounge in her big manicured front yard with her siblings. Occasionally Jimmy's Aunt Dolores Hall (Jimi's mother's sister) came to visit Xenobia's mom, her good friend.

Xenobia is the first person to tell me she was never that impressed with Hendrix as a guitar player. For that reason alone she had to be in this book.

What she brought besides her lifelong bewilderment at the rapture Hendrix invokes in others is a magnificently layered and textured account of the Black community in Seattle of the 1950s and 1960s that spawned our hero.

I was born in Seattle, Washington, but my parents had migrated from the Southwest in the '40s. My father's from Lubbock, Texas, and my mother's from Oklahoma City. My father settled in Seattle with some friends after they were discharged from the navy. My mother had come to Seattle looking for a better lifestyle and job in the major industrial assembly lines like Lockheed and Boeing, who had put out a call for labor. Before she came to Seattle she was only able to get a job as a housekeeper. She was married to somebody else when she moved up there but she ended up marrying my father and starting a family.

I have a younger brother, Joseph Maury, and older and younger sisters, Joetta and Adrienne, and I'm second to the oldest. We have a niece Sala, who is the golden child of the family. She was like a sister—a child my older sister gave birth to when she was still young and living in our parents' home.

Mostly all the adults in the Black community in Seattle came up from the southwest looking for a better life and ended up living in what's called the Central District, or the southern part of Seattle called Rainer View District, where most of the Blacks and Asians lived. When Black folks were investigating the home buyer's market, the white realtors mostly showed them homes in the Central District.

I was born in the Yessler Terrace Housing Projects a couple of blocks from Chinatown (it's now called the International District), which was also a couple of blocks from where my father worked as a redcap at King Street Railroad Station with a few of his same buddies from the Navy.

Most of the Black folks when they came up moved into the projects, even if they were working. After moving from the projects they bought a home. Initially my father didn't know about the G.I. Bill.

I can remember the day one of our neighbors had a conversation with him over the fence. (In the projects in Seattle you had a yard and a fence. You weren't on top of each other like out here.) Our neighbor, who was using his benefit to go to college to become a doctor, told my father, "Under the G.I. Bill you can buy a home and go to school and all that stuff." Right after that conversation we moved and got a home in "The Valley" of the Central District.

Probably just one percent of the population was Black so just about everybody there knew each other and were like kissing cousins. It was a heartbreaker when us kids found out everybody wasn't really blood kin.

My father was abandoned by his mother when he was fourteen years old. My Grandmother (his mother) had decided to move the family to Artesia, New Mexico, and she told all her children, whoever was late coming home from school would be left. My father was late coming home from school so she left him in Lubbock, Texas, all by himself. So he went over to his next-door neighbor's house and told them what had happened. He was raised from that day on by them like he was their child. These were the people my siblings and I called our grandparents.

When my father got his young family situated in Seattle he started bringing all the folks up north from the old neighborhood in Lubbock, Texas, who'd helped raise him. These and others were some of the kinds of folks that pretty much made up our family: the Hubbards, the Williams, and Marcella (Kitt) Fagan "and them." They would all stay in our house at some time when they arrived in town until they found a place. We thought all these people were related to us but nobody really shared blood.

My mother met Dolores Hall, Jimi's aunt, when they both worked at Fort Lawton Air Force Base. Dolores Hall was a very nice woman who always smiled and had a head full of hair; all the women in that family had a head full of hair. Dolores Hall was a lady like my mother who loved a good cup of coffee and good conversation; they had this bond of kindred spirits who were raising their children together.

In the neighborhood almost all the adults worked at the Boeing plant, the Bethlehem Steel Yards, the shipyards, the hospitals, or on the military bases, Fort Louis and Fort Lotten. They didn't let Black folk work in the department store too much back then unless it was sweeping the floors.

As far as our recreation was concerned, we had these cabaret-style nightclubs and after-hour joints in town, but a lot of people had their own after-hours setup in their homes where they would entertain themselves and their friends.

My family didn't own a piano when I and my younger sister started taking piano lessons. The Freeman family, who lived behind us, had one of the two pianos colored folks owned at that time in our neighborhood, in their basement. John Freeman, Sr. used to leave the door unlocked so my sister and I could practice our music. John Freeman, Sr. was in a band (I cannot recall the name of the band nor can I recall the instrument he played; I think it was the saxophone), but the musicians would rehearse in his basement and when they were finished they would leave all of their instruments set up.

In just about every household there was a musical instrument that was connected in some kind of way to a band. In the Freemans' basement he had this whole setup, this mirrored red leather bar with red leather bar stools and space for the musicians to set up with the piano on the side. It could almost be considered an after-hours joint. The guys would finish their gigs downtown or in other parts of the city and come down there and play until daybreak almost. I could hear them all night long from my bedroom window that faced their house.

We had these clubs called the Checkmate, the Downbeat, and the Black and Tan. Being that Seattle had such a small Black community there was a lot of what they would call mixing going on, white women with the Black men. I didn't realize until I was old enough and went on a date to the Black and Tan Club that it was a place where the Black men would go with their white women and stuff. I didn't realize what the name meant until I went to the ladies room and saw that I was the only Black woman in there. Billy Preston, Quincy Jones, and Ray Charles all played there a lot.

Folks would also rent out space and party in some of the smaller halls like the Chamber of Commerce building, the Elks Lodge, or the Masonic Temple. They would have cabaret-style dances with entertainers like James Brown or Ike and Tina Turner. Most of the entertainment was brought in by independent Black producers.

My mother would babysit for this producer named Larry Bailey (same plantation, no kin), one of the main producers for these shows. It wasn't until the "Century 21 World's Fair" came in the mid '60s that they built this huge indoor auditorium called the Seattle Center—a convention center, where these producers were able to produce and promote large sell-out shows like Sly and the Family Stone, Kool and the Gang, and the Motown Revue. (Local bands would be booked for an evening called "The Battle of the Bands," where you could either sit and listen to the music or dance.)

It's so amazing that, as small as the Black community was, whenever they had these shows it was crowded. Black folks from Renton, Tacoma, and Portland, Oregon, would come through. The sportscaster Ahmad Rashad, who was from Tacoma, will tell you to this day that Seattle was like his Los Angeles or Las Vegas.

There was this thing the out-of-town guys used to do for transportation to these weekend functions. They would go to these junkyards that would sell a car for fifty to a hundred dollars. All the guys would pitch in together to get the car and put enough gas in to get you where you were going. If it fell apart, it didn't matter. You'd find another fifty dollars or so and go back home.

Ahmad's crew were mostly his cousins, Charles Mitchell, Mason Mitchell, and "them." They were these "fine," bad-ass football players. He was the only one whose career took off, but all of them are halfway running the city now. Charles Mitchell is the president of Seattle Community College. They were "*fine*," "bad," hard-working brothers who were always looking for a good time whenever they came to party. It was *on* as soon as they came through the door.

Being that Seattle was so small, after a concert we'd all be able to get on the tour bus with the performers and go to the after-parties. There just weren't that many people to inquire about making an after-party.

The drug scene and the sabotage of the Black Cultural Movement busted all that up in the mid '60s. When that whole psychedelic thing started and *Superfly* and the Blaxploitation films took over the minds in the hood, that's when the Funk Culture that we knew just started falling apart.

I didn't notice until I came to the east coast that California and Seattle have a whole other jazz sound of their own. I think Quincy Jones captured a lot of that sound in his earlier music, "Killer Joe," "Mellow Madness." Ooh, it was mellow. Real mellow. A lot of them guys weren't recorded, but I can remember going to a club called the Checkmate that was on 23rd Street, where they had live local music.

This one time I thought the whole club was just about to take off somewhere. This one guy who I went to school with named Vernon Russell used to play the flute, and it was like heaven to hear him this one night. It was a mixed-generation crowd, kind of like it was when we would be playing music with our parents and their friends at home. There would be guys my father's age up there playing. Musicians would leave the stage and someone else would get up and finish what the last one started; it seemed like the sound was never supposed to stop, real chemistry happening in that space. Those musicians were working their "Mojo." I didn't want that sound to ever stop. I wanted the night to last forever. That was the night I discovered the vibrational properties in music outside of the church experience. It was a glorious thing to behold. It was like I was filled to a point where I didn't need to eat no more, didn't want to sleep no more, didn't want to go outside. I didn't even want the sun to rise, because it was dark in the club, and I thought the sunlight would alter the whole atmosphere and break the spell and I would be released from that moment of musical rapture. Man, if they could have recorded the fullness of that music.

Music was the strongest cultural base that we had there. Some people would say the church, but everybody wasn't in the church.

Jimi's Aunt Dolores lived on a hill about three blocks from us. All three of her daughters, Roberta, Julia, and Dee Dee, and her two sons, Robert and Eddy, were about the same age as me and my siblings back then. Whenever your parents would come visit, they'd bring the whole crew.

Sometimes Jimi would come over to our place with his brother Leon, and we would all be sitting on our porch and talking or whatever. We had a big yard, and the best spot for riding our bikes and getting into the fruit trees (cherry, apple, and pear) or the berry bushes (blackberry and raspberry) in the summertime. I think I remember Leon as the only one that would eat the apples; the rest of us would throw them at each other.

I really don't know where Jimi's mother lived. I don't remember ever seeing her. I remember my mother would tell us kids that after Jimi's mother passed, Jimi would always ask why he couldn't go to her funeral. I would ask that same thing.

I met Mr. Hendrix several times. The Black community lived on a level of hills we called the Valley. My family lived on the middle level of the Valley. Jimi and his dad lived deeper down, like Bruce Lee and his family. [Hendrix and Lee not only grew up in the same neighborhood but share a birthday, November 27, which astrologers appropriately describe as "the Day of Electrifying Excitement."]

Bruce Lee went to the same elementary school and high school I went to, though not at the same time. Garfield High School was Black, Asian, Native American, and white. The teachers were mostly white. We had a jazz band that was really good, always the best in the state. Our music department was the strongest department in the school next to sports. Visual arts was a sorry scene at Garfield High School—it wasn't happening at all up in there.

There were a lot of guitar players, but I don't remember seeing guitar in the organized band instruction in the school. Maybe in the jazz band. But a lot of the guys I grew up with who played guitar weren't taking any formal lessons. There was this one guy, Willie Ballard, who was the baddest guitar player in the whole neighborhood. You'd only hear him in his house. I don't think he even made it to clubs. He and Jimi and all these guys would all just be down there playing. Whenever we had to go to the store, we'd pass this pink house with the white porch. The door would be wide open with no screen door and a bunch of them would be in there jamming.

I think that's where they got it together. That's where everybody got their chords together. That's one thing I learned about music from back home: once you learned your chords, you could play anything. None of them wanted to learn how to read or write music because they thought they would lose something they couldn't get back in the process. They felt they didn't need that. Gutbucket blues was the style. I guess you could call it some sort of praising blues. The kind of blues you play when you are thankful for the joy you have, but you just can't enjoy it. It was a lot of twanging and speaking in unknown chords.

There's this church in Seattle called the House of Refuge, Church of God and Christ, located on 23rd Avenue across the street from Garfield High School. It was pastored by Bishop Casey, who really had the power of the word, and it was a sanctified church.

They had this one young man named Keith Barrel who was about fourteen years old—talent in our communities springs up like that—who played the steel guitar, and his sound was very filling, it was that praising-blues sound, it was the sound of home I've yet to experience anywhere else. In his sound you didn't hear a definite distinction between gospel and blues and jazz. It would just take you. Whatever would happen would happen.

Anywhere you'd see Keith, you'd see his whole family. He had a very close family who seemed to really enjoy being together. His father, mother, sisters, brother. Even when he was in some really funky joint, they'd be there, the whole crew.

Now when I go home there's not the nurturing and cultivation in the musical community like I once knew. All the clubs are gone. Back then they had places where they just went to jam. All they did in that building was jam into the night straight into the morning. All those places, the Checkmate, the Downbeat, the Black and Tan, all of them are gone now.

The Downbeat was in the basement of this building near Pioneer Square off First Avenue. That was where the mostly white college kids would be partying during the day, after or before classes. When my brother and I were in elementary school we'd take the long way home so we could go past the Downbeat. We used to go by there and look in, and the beatniks, all dressed in black, would be in there dancing to jazz.

My brother and I would say, that's what we want to be when we grow up, beatniks. The whole scene looked so cool. It made me so I couldn't wait to be a teenager, so I could be cool and party in the day.

Willie Ballard knew his chords real nice. He was so in tune with his instrument and had such control of his sound that you wouldn't hear the metal of his strings at all. He would be wailing on that guitar about the night fever; I think he was too young to handle that heavy sound without a mentor. Just waves of pure sound, real vibrant and real full, and he had control of his instrument at any volume. The style of his music was like this renegade-house-on-fire blues. His music went right through you, way past the praising blues: it was more like a tight-jawed blues with an intent. I compare it to if a locomotive hit you at full speed, when you got up from that impact, from that point on you'd move with the same drive as that locomotive. When something like that hits you, you just come out. He had the touch. His medicine was too much for him and no one around us was skilled enough to know how to help him out.

When a musician's vibration meets with another person's vibration and an accord happens, you're not even conscious of that instrument any more, just that generated energy. Willie Ballard could express his muse. He could play anything—whatever his emotion was he could express that. Whatever he would play would ride you on his expressway. He had a musical maturity beyond his years and skill. He was really very special.

I think Jimi was more the one that gave the guitar a voice, and made it articulate, and made it speak in vowels and syllables. He took that aspect further than anyone else.

He was part of a pack of guitar players that was always practicing. The music was always being created. They were either rehearsing, practicing, or performing. A lot of them, though, got caught in what was called the Youth Center for Juvenile Delinquency.

I didn't feel that Jimi was all that special then because he wasn't really the strongest one of all those players. I didn't even know he had got famous. I was in Spanish class in high school and this friend of mine named Michael Preston said he was going to Sicks Stadium (the baseball stadium) to see Jimi play. I said, Jimi don't play baseball. It was hard for me to comprehend him playing there because I'd never even heard of any musicians playing in a baseball stadium and selling it out. I thought, in Seattle it rains, and people are going to buy tickets to see Jimi in a stadium? I couldn't understand it. I didn't know he'd gone away and joined the Air Force and done all this stuff.

I would hear his music on the radio but our reception was very bad so I couldn't quite make the sound out. Everybody was all up in his lyrics and how deep they were with "Purple Haze" and all this step.

Jimi had these boy cousins and I don't even know if these guys are still alive—but the oldest brother we called Butchy. I can't think of his last name. Butchy was in prison when he was a teenager. The other young guys that he hung with behind the wall were about his same age and they were called the Purple Haze Gang by the other inmates. These little young dudes used to terrorize this adult prison, Monroe State Reformatory. I used to go up to the prison with some friends of mine to conduct this "Black Cultural Workshop Behind the Wall" on Saturday that we had put together for the Black population. That's when I would see Butchy and his crew. Butchy had this *fire* in him. When I would talk to him he was always so pleasant, asking about his brothers and mother, always so cordial. Then I would hear these horror stories. I mean these young dudes were terrorizing a state penitentiary. When the guards would send 'em to "the hole"—and they were always going to the hole—it would take five or six guards to take one down. And these were small guys too, short, even—kids!

I couldn't understand Jimi's music on the radio because of the static, but even when I bought his records after he died, I was *trying* to get into what everybody else was into.

I really do like his "Star-Spangled Banner" though.

Craig Street

Courtesy Craig Street

*It would come as a surprise to find out anyone reading this book did not own at least one of the albums Craig Street has produced in the last eight years. Among his fine credits are Cassandra Wilson's **Blue Light Til Dawn** and **New Moon Daughter**, k.d. lang's **Drag**, Javon Jackson's **Pleasant Valley**, Chris Whitley's **Perfect Day**, Susanna Baca's **Eco de Sombras** and **Espiritu Vivo**, Me'Shell NdegéOcello's **Bitter**, Kevin Breit and Cyro Baptista's **Supergenerous**, Joe Henry's **Scar**, Toshi Reagon's **Toshi**, and Chocolate Genius' **Black Music**.*

*In 1989 and 1991 Street produced two all-Hendrix programs of concert music featuring some of the freshest young talents around. The first, **If I Could Get That Sound**, occurred at Town Hall.*

On that date Hendrix was interpreted and re-orchestrated for horns, acoustic piano, and percussion by Oliver Lake, Brandon Ross, Geri Allen, Melvin Gibbs, Mark Letford, Craig Harris, Graham Haynes, and David Torn, among others. Street's second all-Hendrix program featured a piano trio led by jazz pianist Geri Allen with the Bushwick, Brooklyn-born piano prodigies/hiphop MCs Marc and Scott Batson.

Back when he was a popular alternative radio deejay for the Bay Area's Pacifica Station, Street helped produce a twelve-hour documentary on Hendrix for National Public Radio.

We haven't mentioned that he plays blues guitar exceedingly well in various nonstandard tunings.

His formidable knowledge of the modern recording studio's sound-manipulation capacities and Hendrix's contributions to its vocabulary make him an irresistible choice for this book.

In 1966 my family moved from Los Angeles to an area right on the border of Oakland and Berkeley. (My father later taught criminology at U.C. Berkeley.) One of the first things we did as a family there was go to a peace march in Golden Gate Park, where I remember particularly enjoying Buffalo Springfield and Jesse Colin Young.

My junior high school was an all-Black high school where they had started bussing in white kids from across town. There was a fairly tense environment around there, but there was also a lot of strange openness.

Almost immediately I got into an accelerated Environmental Design program, a satellite school within a school. It was run by these two former U.C. Berkeley students and based on the philosophies and teachings of Buckminster Fuller. Ethnically, this program had a pretty diverse population.

Berkeley then was wild, but, in retrospect, it was a really amazing place to grow up. But at the time I didn't like it. It's a very conservative place, actually, and I don't think it was ever so liberal or left as people think of it as being. There was all this strange stuff going on, but the fact that they were bussing kids as late as 1967 says a lot.

I got into another magnet program when I was in high school, and about halfway through the semester all the Black teachers in that school took all the Black students and started a separate school. I loved it.

The school only lasted a couple of years because the city came down on it saying, Hey, we bussed people in, you can't segregate yourselves.

I think what was great about Berkeley, though, was the amount of information I was able to take in. I was twelve and just getting into things, reading *Crawdaddy* and *Rolling Stone,* and because my dad is an audiophile and there was so much music in my house I had to scrounge around to find other stuff.

Radio was ridiculous, a free-for-all. Like you'd turn on the radio at that time and you were likely to hear anything. There was a great soul station that for a brief time opened up, and you'd hear Coltrane, James Brown, and Hendrix. With the FM stations like KSAN and KNPX, now you're talking like the height of late '60s freeform radio.

My dad worked as a consultant for jury selection on Huey Newton's first trial, worked as an adviser to the Panthers on a lot of legal issues, and later with Angela Davis during her trial. As a professor he was also very active in politics—particularly in the Third World strike that went on at U.C. Berkeley around '67, '68.

There were always radicals, Panthers, and other interesting folks in the house, and a lot of people I grew up with were either in the Black Panther party or had older siblings who were in the party. They influenced a lot of attitudes about things, fashion included, and they were definitely a force to be emulated.

Musically, I saw everything.

Bill Graham was just starting up then and he used school kids to distribute posters and flyers. The Berkeley Community Theatre was one of the venues Graham used to put on shows, and my magnet school was in that building. Almost everybody who went to that school worked for Graham, so by the time I was in 9th or 10th grade I went to basically every show.

I'd hear music in little clubs too. I used to walk past a club called Jabberwocky on Telegraph Avenue just north of Ashby. They used to have people like Lightnin' Hopkins and Mance Lipscomb play there all the time. I'd pop in for sound checks because I was too young to get into a show.

I don't remember when I first heard Hendrix. I do remember hearing "Purple Haze" and "Foxy Lady" when they first came out and liking them as real cool songs, but I didn't have the albums.

At the time I was buying a lot of blues records, basic pop stuff, Rolling Stones, the Monkees, rhythm and blues stuff. Hendrix didn't become a major thing with me until around the time of *Band of Gypsys*. Everybody in school had that record.

I was in my first band around that time; I was about fifteen. We played in North Richmond, a small Black community just north of Berkeley, in this club that was owned by this Black motorcycle gang. We did these really long sets, like six sets a night, backing people up like these two little kids, a crooner, this blues guy, and the woman who owned the club who was a shake dancer. In between we'd get our own set. We were playing things like Hendrix tunes, P-funk tunes, Neil Young songs, all the kind of stuff we were all listening to at the time.

The first Hendrix I owned was the Monterey record with Otis Redding on one side and Hendrix on the other. I'd put the Hendrix side on and my dad would be like, "Man, what are you playing that for? Put the other side on."

I totally fell in love with Dylan at age nine or ten and Dylan was one of the few points where me and my dad agreed musically. The first record I ever bought was Dylan's *Bringing It All Back Home*. I remember hearing Hendrix's version of "Like a Rolling Stone" and thinking, This is unbelievable. I tried to pick it out on my little nylon string guitar and figuring out, Oh, he must be detuning. I remember trying to decipher all the stuff he was saying in between the songs, like, What the hell?

That was the only Hendrix I owned for a long time. Then I got *Smash Hits* because I liked the cowboy outfits they were wearing.

Hendrix was probably the one guy in '67, '68 that I didn't see in concert—not even those legendary Winterland Ballroom shows I heard so much about. But he did a show at the Berkeley

Community Theatre, May 30, 1970, which was really amazing for a lot of reasons.

Berkeley was basically in a state of war. The National Guard was there, and there had been riots going on for weeks.

In an effort to defuse things they were letting a lot of people into this show, even though it was sold out. I remember being at the back door and somebody associated with the band letting a lot of people in. I remember going to the front of the stage, the pit, just as Hendrix was coming out. All I remember is just this sensation of being pinned to the wall. The power of the music was insane.

The band was Mitchell and Cox. Hendrix wasn't doing a lot of jumping around, he was just standing there playing.

I had been to lot of jazz things with my dad and had seen Miles Davis and Roland Kirk, a lot of amazing people. My musical taste was skewed when it came to pop. I was like, it's cool or whatever, but it's not like Buddy Guy or Miles Davis or Coltrane. I was looking for things like that, and seeing Hendrix was my first time at a rock concert hearing something that wasn't jazz that had me distinctly thinking, This is like Miles or Coltrane. It was an absolute fulcrum point in terms of recognizing that there was something greater going on here than the media would have me believe.

I used to devour articles about Hendrix in *Rolling Stone* or *Guitar Player,* and none of them really prepared me for actually seeing this guy. It was really clear to me at this point that this was someone who was an really amazing musician. I became a fiend for bootlegs, especially of that whole period of '69, '70, where he was really stretching musically.

One of the difficult things Hendrix presents as a musical entity and as a human being is that he broke all the rules, all of them. All the rules about what is to be a Black man, a rock and roll star, a pop musician. Up until Hendrix, and with all due respect to the

Beatles, there was never anybody in rock who'd attained his level of musicianship. He was at the level of the great jazz or improvisatory artists that were around like an Ali Akbar Khan or a Coltrane.

A lot of the controversy about Hendrix that has come from people in so-called proper musical worlds, like the classical world or the conservative side of jazz, has to do with people saying there's no way that this guy coming from the background he came from could be on a par with a Miles Davis or a Coltrane.

I think the fact that Roland Kirk, Miles, and Larry Young recognized Hendrix as a musical peer was an acknowledgment that this guy was in fact someone whose coordination of imagination and technical ability was unparalleled.

People will frequently ask me, "What's the difference between Hendrix and Jeff Beck, Eric Clapton, or Eddie Van Halen?" Well, Hendrix to me is something like Robert Johnson—a traveling blues guy who at some point took a chunk of time to develop exponentially.

From a mythological point of view, people like to say Johnson disappeared and sold his soul to the devil. The reality is the guy was traveling round listening to everything—Skip James, Charlie Patton, Lonnie Johnson. There are stories of him playing polkas and country music, whatever people wanted to hear. He had the foresight to ignore lines and barriers and borders and to push things together with an amazing sense of poetry. His use of language was phenomenal and, combined with his capacity to perform, everything he used got fused into something else.

Well, Hendrix, in the same way, would play with whoever would have him, and had a diverse record collection. Whatever Hendrix heard, he'd scoop right up.

There are all these accounts of how when he first went to England, Jeff Beck told Pete Townsend, "This guy Hendrix is stealing all your stuff." But Hendrix had heard the Yardbirds, and what Townsend and Beck were doing with feedback, and he'd heard Clapton too, but he had no boundaries. Whatever he heard would come out. In today's terminology he'd be called eclectic. Well, it's not eclectic. It's just somebody that didn't have any borders.

So here's a country song, "The Wind Cries Mary," which is like Hank Williams's "I'm So Lonesome I Could Cry," and then there's something else with a weird sonic thing like John Cage or somebody. Only it's not pretentious. It's not somebody sitting down from an intellectual standpoint and saying, "Let's try this." It's just unfettered free expression. That's something that's very difficult to harness and to focus on, and it placed him so far above everybody else.

This is also somebody who was a consummate songwriter. The reason we listen today is because those are great songs and Hendrix was an unbelievable vocalist and lyricist, ridiculous guitarist, he had all of these things together. Most people don't have that. There's always something that's slightly lacking.

People who don't have it all together usually get with other people who are slightly lacking. Like you listen to Led Zeppelin. If you take the individual elements, none of them are particularly strong on their own, but here are four guys who had the sense to bond together and form something powerful.

The popular thing for people to think about with Hendrix was what would happen if he had musicians who were at his level or higher so that he could elevate his game. He never had any musicians who could push him.

What he did have by the time of that Berkeley show were two incredibly supportive and sympathetic musicians backing him up. He got the solid rhythmic foundation he needed from Billy Cox and he got that over-the-edge sonic thing he needed from Mitch Mitchell.

He was able to fill in the space in between because he had a profound understanding of how to make a three-piece sound incredibly huge. Of how a certain approach to bass will fill in the things that the guitar only hints at. What's fantastic about Hendrix is that you always think you're hearing more than what's actually there. When you analyze it there's an impression that this guy is playing this huge chord. He might only be playing three notes, but there are these overtones and harmonics and sonic things that are all happening too.

Hendrix was also a great producer and it's really evidenced with the stuff he produced outside of his own stuff. He was also able to get these sounds on really primitive devices, really limited means.

Today some of the things Hendrix spent hours trying to do you can do with the flick of a switch. If you want to record backward you just push a button—you don't have to flip the tape around. Like at that point they had to literally take a reel of tape and turn it upside down and around. This isn't even mentioning what you can do with computers now.

Technology has always moved rapidly. All the records that came out in 1967 like *Sgt Pepper* and *Are You Experienced* were recorded on four-track machines. The density they have is because they bounced between machines and did submixes: fill up all four tracks, do a submix to another machine, then start building up on that machine and bounce to another one. Well, that requires an incredible amount of thinking ahead. In the process of doing submixes something is going to have to shift. This is why on a lot records from that time the bass or drums are off to one side. The question becomes: what am I going to have to do with EQ so that this third-generation bounce-mix holds up? Because you can't go back. If it gets undone you have to start all over again.

The digital age isn't quite sophisticated enough or perfected enough yet to translate what comes from analog tape. Analog is still probably the most perfect storage medium for music because of what it's capable of soaking up harmonically and how that relates to our physicality and how we hear music. Digital is just math and the sampling rate simply isn't high enough once you start looking at human frequency response relative to the sampling rate and not just sine waves, which is what the companies that manufacture CDs look at.

Human beings can basically hear above a decibel level of 20 kilocycles but our bodies pick up information outside of that. We feel high-end information up to about 60 kilocycles and we feel low-end information down to about 3 or 4 hertz. We feel it through our bones, through our skin, and through our body cavities. So when people who've heard things like vinyl or tape or live music hear a CD it sounds pretty limited, to put it mildly. Because there's all this harmonic information that's been cut off.

In the early '60s there were a lot of technical things that had to be gone into then. People at that point in time were really discovering a lot about sound as they got past the engineers, the lab guys with suits and ties who were in a union. You hear stories about the Beatles's guy, Geoff Emerick, having to get a special waiver to use a microphone in front of the kick drum. The only reason they were able to do that was because the Beatles were selling tons of records, but nobody had ever done that kind of experimentation. All these things that are simple to do, like flangeing, which was at that point where somebody puts their thumb on the machines to get them slightly out of whack with one another and give you this swooshing sound.

The rules those engineers lived by had a lot to do with things like Hendrix's disappointment with the original mastering of *Electric Ladyland.* He'd worked hard to get these phasing effects— these things that happened when you get the same overdubbed sounds to go out of phase with one another—not quite 180 degrees but more like 160 degrees. That's how you get these sounds where if you're listening in stereo it sounds like something is coming from behind your head or hovering on the outside of the speaker. With *Electric Ladyland,* which was saturated with those kinds of effects, they took it to the mastering house and the technicians heard it and said, "Oh, it's out of phase," and click, they "fixed" it. Which meant when it came back, it sounded flat!

People wonder if Hendrix heard that way because of the drugs he was using. I think the way creative impulses can be made to open up can take a lot of different forms. It's quite possible that some of those people who were creating those sounds were using drugs. The difficulty I have with that, is OK, it's a fair enough area to go into, but it's not of much interest unless it's in the first person. So if there's a bunch of stuff with Hendrix saying, "I had this particular hallucinogenic experience and I heard this," or, "It got me seeking after this," then fine. But with Black creative people there's a tendency to ignore the really hard work that goes on.

I remember, even as a youth, being really pissed off with how with Hendrix, it always seemed that people were only looking at these over-the-top aspects of what his life was supposed to be about. But what you hear consistently from his friends and people around him is that the guy never put a guitar down. That's also what everybody says about Parker and Coltrane, who was, like, practicing fourteen hours a day. When you look at Hendrix's tour schedule and him playing in the studio all the time, it's like at some point somebody has to sit back and say, "This is somebody who worked really hard at their craft."

Yes, there's a God-given gift, a natural talent and a blessing that can't be denied—but saying that he just came from another planet undermines the humanness that's there in the work. The humanity that's involved in somebody being able to dig down that deep, pull it out, and, against all odds, put it out there for the world to hear. The kind of tremendous effort that has proven itself over time to be dangerous and fatal for many who do it. To wrench that degree of emotional and spiritual truth out of yourself is no small task.

There are still these myths that Hendrix was a drug addict who died of an overdose at age 27. He wasn't an addict nor did he die of an overdose, but it's almost like this is a way to defuse the research and the work of someone who played music all of his life. Someone who learned from his time on the road and got fired from bands for experimenting on the road.

He wasn't somebody who was able to reap the benefits of longevity in his quest to develop his craft. So it's not like George Nakashima who had years to develop his craft in making his furniture, or a Frank Gehry. Finally, now, after years of people saying, "This guy is out of his mind," it's suddenly, "Wow, he might be one of the greatest architects ever." But Gehry has had the benefit of time and technology. He can draw a wacky curve and have a computer program designed to make fighter planes translate the kind of structure or framework necessary for those curves to exist.

Hendrix never had the benefit of seeing that sort of fruition.

Still, it's amusing to consider that we haven't really come that far from what he was able to do with the most basic things, an amplifier and a guitar and his hands. We've made it simpler so that you don't have to sweat as much, but all of what he accomplished with basic technology is infused in what we do.

What's amazing about those recordings is the sense of opposites that exist: dry against wet, near against far. Having a room sound contrast with the reverb from a spring or a plate or a tape echo.

It's like cooking, where you have these different elements that give it the taste, that give it the flavor, that make it an experience—no pun intended—for those who are going to feast on this delightful aural meal.

SLIGHT RETURN

So the fire and the ferocity of Jimi Hendrix endure for reasons that have little to do with hippie nostalgia, radical-protest romance, or rockstar flash. Though born in time to experience the fabled and exuberant uprisings and conflagrations of the 1960s, Hendrix remains irreducible to the status of Woodstock relic or rebel-youth touchstone. We keep Hendrix close because he remains as much a contemporary as a classic. He haunts this time as sardonically as he did his own; and his sound remains the touchstone: of things being born and things falling apart, of the glitch heard round the world and the suicide bomb rocketing above the din of the disco floor.

As Street and Drayton's testimonies attest (and those of Miles Davis, Ornette Coleman, and Rahsaan Roland Kirk confirm), Hendrix was a *musician's musician's* musician. The guy who impressed the guys who impress all the other guys. A guy responsible for one of the most readily identifiable and widely (when not tritely) imitated sounds of the twentieth century. A sound as familiar and flavorful to modern ears as the scatsongs of Louis Armstrong and the wounding horn of Miles Davis. Like Armstrong's and Davis's, Hendrix's sound emphatically declares that the vagaries of human experience have been supremely, sublimely concentrated into an energized packet of racket by a staunch individualist and master musical filterer. One who'll fire that packet through a pressure valve—nay, a supercollider—fully intending for it explode on contact with our goosebumped skin, feverish greymatter, and prehensile brainstems for maximum race-memory igniting impact.

When we speak of such musicians having a tone all their own, we mean all has been stripped away but their essence, their signature embellishments of punctuation and parable. And whether that musician is the Armstrong–Miles–Hendrix triumvirate or the Coltrane–Nusrat Khan–Milton Nascimento tripartite or the Wonder–Marley–Santana trinity, what we discover in their tone quality is a pithy storytelling vehicle designed for evocative travels through every musical culture on the planet. Hendrix is a global phenomenon and we all live in his sound universe now, wherever music and electricity come together.

His heady encounters with the world's race, sex, style, and technology conflamma left the world louder, brighter, and boomier than the world he was born into. He obliterated the distinction between music and noise, aural pleasure and pain, and we've all been paying the price ever since. Heavy metal, Digital Dolby Sound—just blame Hendrix. You think would we have to put up with all that had he never been born? Except for Hendrix, louder was not just better, but a wormhole, a gateway, an interdimensional portal to the same place where Sun Ra, Albert Ayler, and Coltrane took the muse Noise in their pursuits of a "Cosmic Music"; except the ecumenical Hendrix wanted to pursue a path to cosmos that would be accessible to the average

American Pop fan. Unity in destruction, symmetry in chaos: these were his hallmarks. It's why the same man who wanted you to never hear surf music again could speak of taking you to the methane seas of Jupiter. In Yoruba philosophy they eschew notions of good and evil in favor of speaking of constructive and destructive forces, forces that build up and forces that tear down. Hendrix moved along this axis freely.

The now-clichéd notion of music as melted architecture takes on a literal cast in Hendrix. Not because his vision was hallucinogenically inspired, but because of how preoccupied this superlative expressionist and sonic architect was with building up and then vaporizing traditional songform and structure. He once described the sound he heard in his head and couldn't quite get out as a Bach–flamenco–Muddy Waters kind of thing—rolling into one the world, the flesh, and the celestial order of things.

Erotic and cosmic aspirations always seem to be vying for attention in Hendrix's lyrics and music. The forces of nature and nurture; wine, woman, song, and spirit; sex, drugs, rock and roll, and the holy ghost are always all right there, visibly, suggestively, seductively, bubbling on the surface of a Hendrix performance. So too are the vaster regions known to motivate human curiosity: oceans, stars, planets, galaxies, waterfalls, fire-red moons. Sound-painting was a favorite Hendrix description of his ambient music. Sound as canvas, as primer and oils, as brushes and knives.

As Vernon Reid has intimated about "Machine Gun," his cry of love for fallen soldiers everywhere, the theme of the song is embodied in the projected images of the improvisation.

Craig Street is provocatively fond of citing Hendrix as one of the great twentieth-century composers, and if there is anyone who has reproduced what that century screamed like more accurately than Hendrix, let him now step forth. Of course to

even consider Hendrix under the banner of the much bally-
hooed term *composer* brings us back to the problem of race and
recognition in a country where Black people are still rarely
given credit for intellectual capacity or conceptual contributions. Old fantasies about the Negro brain being less evolved
than that of whites still prevail, having changed little since
Thomas Jefferson's infamous utterances on the subject.

Some of this underestimation derives from racism. Some of
it also derives from how African American creativity is so omniv-
orously American in its counter-institutional refusal to wait for
state approval before storming the grounds and barricades of
our cultural gatekeepers. Hendrix acknowledged African and
Native American influences on his work—rhythmically, melodi-
cally, and spiritually. The brandishing of so-called folk forms
within cosmopolitan musical conceptions is a hallmark of twentieth-century music, from Stravinsky, Bartok, and Cage to
Coltrane, Motown, and the Art Ensemble of Chicago. Hendrix's
reworking of his roots was less academic but no less scholarly,
judicious, and lyrically disruptive of the status quo. His disturbance of same also cut mercilessly across hard and fast musical
categories. For this reason he would find himself frowned upon
by older blues musicians, rhythm-and-blues peers, and even
champions of free jazz like Amiri Baraka and A. B. Spellman—
who once, in conversation with the author, made a disparaging
comparison between Hendrix's tone and Albert Ayler's, describ-
ing Jimi's as "ugly" and Albert's as "beautiful."

The unwillingness to accept boundaries between the music
he heard in his head and the high and low forms of the day is
what makes Hendrix's contribution so deafeningly successful in
the end and so damned difficult to lay to rest. The best of
American culture is chauvinistically multicultural, mongrelized,
and bastardized, smelted rather than melted down into some
homegrown stew peppered with highly personal seasonings.

Hendrix now seems like the summation of the '60s, as each of his major appearances of the decade—Monterey in 1967, Woodstock in '69, Band of Gypsys on New Year's Eve that same year—have come to symbolize in broad strokes the quick transition from psychedelic freefall to edenic communalism to the short death march that wound the counterculture's youthdance down to the creepy cocaine crawl and drawl you hear in Sly Stone's *There's a Riot Goin' On*. All of those performances, Hendrix's own first and last stands, also represent Hendrix changing the segregated faces of rock and roll and rhythm and blues, setting the stage not only for the big tents of David Bowie and Led Zeppelin but for the socially conscious, sonically expansive soul music that began flooding forth from Stevie Wonder, Marvin Gaye, Curtis Mayfield, Earth Wind and Fire, and Funkadelic following his death. Not to mention Miles Davis and company: Wayne Shorter, Joe Zawinul, Herbie Hancock, John McLaughlin, and Chick Corea all moved to jack in, turn up, and rock out.

Hendrix took the majestic wail of the storefront gospel singer and the eviscerating, stratosphere-seeking honks and shouts of barwalking soul saxophonists, and married them to the most earthbound of American musics, the Delta blues. This is why in Hendrix we hear this strange mixture of Jackie Wilson's eerily effeminate machismo, Pharaoh Sanders's heaven-renting screeches, and the taildragging, dirt-slithering serpentine fire of a John Lee Hooker, a Lightning Hopkins. So scars and scares are prevalent in the Hendrix sound. Yet so is the desire for a redemptive waterworld—blatantly heard in *Electric Ladyland*'s epic-length underwater sonata, "1983 . . . A Merman I Should Turn to Be," in *Are You Experienced*'s "May This Be Love," *The Cry of Love*'s "Drifting," and *Axis: Bold As Love*'s "Castles Made of Sand."

His striving toward a unity of the primal and the conceptual mark him as one of the grand unifying figures of twentieth-century creativity—kin to Stravinsky, Picasso, Kahlo, Miles, and Basquiat.

That he rammed his persona through sophisticated, home-made mutant forms keeps Hendrix from ever seeming out-moded or outdated.

Artists who write themselves into the canon through force of will tend to be prodigious and hyperproductive. This seems especially to have been the case with Hendrix and Basquiat, who seemed to have known their time here was extremely lim-ited. Hendrix's work ethic would see him re-record a minor rhythm guitar part forty and fifty times before becoming satis-fied, always seeking the telling nuance from the smallest ges-ture. Reminding of the Wayne Shorter who accounted for his own attention to sculptural detail in composition by saying, "You can have a penny without a million dollars but you can't have a million dollars without a penny. If the penny ain't in there it's jive." From Hendrix we expect flamboyancy, but the poetic detail, the pennies, stun us just as much.

We marvel that Hendrix evolved as quickly as he did from *Are You* to *Axis* to *Electric Lady* to *Band of Gypsys* to *Cry of Love* in the blink-and-you'll-miss-it span of four years. The depth of field of his productions, the swirling miasma of forms, recon-textualize our ears at every turn, putting funk and etheric com-ponents together in bewildering, elegant ways. Hendrix brought the funky bass into rock as surely as he brought edgy experi-mentation into staid soul music.

The virtue of the accident so prized in a lot of twentieth-cen-tury music gets raised to virtuoso levels in the rock and roll of Jimi Hendrix. In his hands a host of effects once considered to be just plain wrong or at best tacky—squawking feedback, out-of-phase mastering, and so forth—go on to become the lingua franca of modernity and melody.

Like all great artists, Hendrix worked long and hard to realize the sound-paintings he heard in his head and to create a delivery system that could capture listeners of disparate degrees of education and sophistication. Per hiphop MC Rakim Allah, we have been the journal and Hendrix has been the journalist. So that three decades after his departure our inner ears, our freaking cochleas, have got Hendrix graffiti scrawled, nay, crawling all over them. Especially if we worship at the altar of the electric guitar.

There are electric guitar players we love because they so blatantly bring Hendrix to mind in size, scale, woofwarpwhang, and volume—Ted Nugent, Robin Trower, Neal Schon, Eddie Van Halen, Steve Vai, Vernon Reid. There are others we adore because they remind us so little of Hendrix—James Blood Ulmer, Allan Holdsworth, Thurston Moore, Derek Bailey, Keith Richards, George Harrison, Sonny Sharrock, Bill Frisell, Keith Rowe, Keith Levene, Andy Gill, George Benson, Morgan Craft. There are the rare birds who bring as much fire to the wood as Jimi but are so much their own man as to mask the influence behind what event-singularities they set off as soloists: Jeff Beck, Duane Allman, John McLaughlin, Eddie Hazel, Carlos Santana, Pete Cosey, David Fiuczynski, Rene Akhan. Then there are those who operate somewhere in between, fellow researchers with a likeminded passion for melding melodious chords and the odd sound—Jimmy Page, Marlo Henderson, Ronnie Drayton, The Edge, Eddie Van Halen (yeah him again), Andy Summers, Dr. Know, David Byrne, Adrian Belew, Marc Ribot, Kurt Cobain, Billy Corgan, Kevin Breit, Kirk Douglas.

The funny thing is, Hendrix seems to have presaged them all at one point or another—the blatant, the mutants, the blenders, the unborn—as by the same token, Jimi's Dalí-drippy cup spilleth over with the aged bourbon taste of all who preceded him in prominence, if not time—Charlie Christian; Django Reinhardt; B.B., Freddy, and Albert King; T-Bone Walker; Guitar Slim; Johnny Guitar Watson; Hubert Sumlin; Earl and John Lee Hooker; Chuck Berry; Scotty Moore; Buddy Holly; Les Paul; Grant Green; Wes Montgomery; Steve Cropper.

It's not hard—no stretch at all—to hear Hendrix echoed in Miles Davis's wah-wah and the synthesizers of Herbie Hancock, Josef Zawinul, Bernie Worrell, and Stevie Wonder or the violin of Jean-Luc Ponty or the flute of James Newton, the saxophone of David Murray, the cornets of Butch Morris and Graham Haynes; or to back-project his stank onto the prior emissions of Sun Ra, Albert Ayler, John Coltrane, Joe Henderson, Eric Dolphy, Marshall Allen, John Gilmore, Lester Bowie, the Edgar Varèse of *Ionisation*, the Karlheinz Stockhausen of *Sternklang*, the Claude Debussy of *Le Mer*, the Beethoven of the Ninth Symphony; or to underscore the links between his long-form, eclectic, stereophonic statements and *Stand, Bitches Brew, Shaft, Superfly, What's Goin On, Heroes, Dark Magus, Music for Airports, My Life in the Bush of Ghosts, He Loved Him Madly, Mothership Connection, The Motor-Booty Affair, Remain in Light, Discipline, It Takes a Nation of Millions to Hold Us Back, Three Feet High and Rising, Paul's Boutique, Ready to Die, The Chronic, What Does Your Shadow Look Like, Only Built 4 Cuban Linx, Superunknown, Blue Light Til Dawn* (to name but a paltry Afro-American-leaning few).

If I was allowed but one Hendrix album to accompany me in my travels it would be *Axis: Bold As Love*. It is at once the most personal, whimsical, reckless, and inscrutable of his recordings and, except for "Little Wing" and "Spanish Castle Magic," the one with the fewest anthologized songs. It begins apocalyptically and playfully with "EXP" and "Up from the Skies" and ends in New Jerusalem splendor with the song that gives the disc its title. The space in between is full of breaking hearts and romantic balladry, and imagery worthy of Percy Bysshe Shelley: a panoply of butterflies and moonbeams, fairy tales and gold-and-rose-colored dream angels, Indian braves who die unheralded in their sleep, suicidal cripples saved by serendipitous golden-winged ships, aphrodisiacs masquerading as dragonflies. You can call it Hendrix's *Lord of the Rings* album, and I won't get mad at ya. *Axis* is also the album where you can spend hours trying to figure out how to move from one loopy 9th or major 7th chord to the next with the proper hammer-on/pull-off finesse while simultaneously thumbing a bass progression. It's the album where Hendrix made rhythm-guitar playing more complicated than anyone since Blind Willie McTell and Blind Gary Davis and lead overtures more orchestral than we've heard in anybody's pop music since, Brian May barely notwithstanding.

If *Are You Experienced* is the shock of the new and *Electric Ladyland* the shape of things to come, *Axis* is Hendrix as Stravinsky—strange composer in a strange land, reinventing rock and roll as he went along, earth, moon, and starry-eyed song. It is also the album where Mitch Mitchell and Hendrix seem to have scored every hit, roll, snap, stroke, ride, crash, and paradiddle to function like some newfangled notion of percussive harmony for every lyric epiphany, guitar detonation, and neighing, feedback-wracked orgasmic climax.

Musicians come and musicans go. New genres rise up to claim the space in our hearts occupied by old ones, as those in turn get swallowed by the Next Big Thing to tickle our neophiliac listening fancy. And then there are the verities and holy trinities—Monk, Ellington, Mingus. Armstrong, Parker, Coltrane. Robert Johnson, Son House, Skip James. Sun Ra, Miles Davis, George

Clinton. Wonder, Gaye, and Green. James Brown, Sly Stone, Curtis Mayfield. Dylan, the Beatles, the Rolling Stones. Iggy, Bowie, the Sex Pistols. Bad Brains, Living Colour, Fishbone.

And then there's James. Who somehow manages to hit all the notes they hit and then some. Who we never need to go back to because he seems not to have ever departed. I joked with a friend recently that the reason we keep buying every repackaged greatest hits, outtakes, and false starts compilation is because we like to imagine that it's really a new Jimi Hendrix album.

Hendrixian. What we ought to mean when we say love never dies and Jimi springs eternal.

The Alternative and Prognosticative Histories of James Marshall Hendrix

It has become de rigeur to speculate on what Hendrix might have done had he lived into the '70s, '80s, '90s, and beyond. To speculate on what collaborations with the first wave of Black Rock bands might have yielded—Isley Brothers, Bar-Kays, WAR, Mandrill, Funkadelic, Rufus featuring Chakha Khan, Mother's Finest, Maxayn, Graham Central Station, Labelle, Earth Wind and Fire. To wonder whether he and his guitar and songwriting idol, Curtis Mayfield, would have got something going. To imagine Jimi on *Soul Train* backing up Al Green or Stevie Wonder.

With pop music becoming increasingly segregated in the '70s—as hard rock and metal became commercially codified as "white boy music" and funk became understood as a "brother-thang"—Hendrix might have functioned as a bridge between the musical clash of race worlds.

Would he have followed others of his generation, like Dylan, Neil Young, and Joni Mitchell, into more acoustic-oriented stylings? Would he and Stevie Wonder have begun spending long hours together in Electric Lady studios, where Stevie spent months creating *Music of My Mind, Talking Book, Inner Visions, Fulfillingness' First Finale,* and *Songs in the Key of Life*? Would the advent of fusion have found him more in the company of Miles Davis, Gil Evans, Tony Williams, Chick Corea, and Wayne Shorter? Or that of Sun Ra, The Art Ensemble of Chicago, Anthony Braxton? Would the advent of glam, Bowie, Iggy, The New York Dolls, and KISS have inspired him to reconsider the outrageous spectacle of rock and roll theatre he was largely starting to abandon in pursuit of musical seriousness? What might he and Patti Smith and Richard Hell have gotten into? Or David Byrne and Brian Eno? Or Michael Jackson and Prince? Or, Jah only knows, Bob Marley and The Wailers? The possibilities are infinite, staggering to speculate about, but then again, not. There's something satisfying in the way the world and the musicians who follow a master like Hendrix learned from him the value of their own cadence and to sing their own timeless songs in their own voice. For all we know music, per The Twins, may have gotten all it needed from Hendrix and let him move on. For all we know that may be a load of crap, some airy-fairy, pie-in-the-sky stuff too. But what are we who love Hendrix if not a nation of stardusted dreamers?

I have often been given to wonder what a highly evolved creative imagination like Hendrix's might have come up with had he worked in other mediums. What would a Jimi Hendrix novel have read like? What would a Jimi Hendrix film have looked like?

In the course of imagining such works, I've crafted some Borgesian fluff for this occasion, confections turned fictions filled with my own humble, hobbled together answers to those curious questions. Read on at my own peril.

from The Jimi Hendrix Omnibus, *containing the novella* Electric Ladyland, *the* Axis: Bold As Love *diaries, and all the short fiction originally published in the collections* Are You Experienced, Smash Hits, Band of Gypsys *and* Cry of Love

Electric Ladyland, a novella in fourteen chapters

...And the Gods Made Love

The bed would be bloody. Filled with all the blood his body contained, all that remained pouring forth as they performed the sex rite for the last time. A bloody death that transported the seeds of its own resurrection from his carrion flesh to her fertile mortal soil. A child gonna be born. Gonna be a son of a gun.

Have You Ever Been (To Electric Ladlyland?)

22 points in her body had been pierced. Today they all felt like heating coils or lightning rods. It was as if she had castrated her babydaddy at the moment of his demise and laid his excised member up in her belly for nine months. Up there it had been gathering steam, forming thunderclouds, crackling the condensed air with high-voltage currents.

Crosstown Traffic

The babydaddy's twin brother wanted her to marry him, then sign adoption papers before the baby was born. He had no blood on his hands, only survivor guilt. He believed it was his obligation to marry her. He knew that winning her heart would not be so simple a matter as merely resembling her dead and buried babydaddy. His need for redemption was strong, though, and could only be fulfilled through his dead brother's woman.

She categorically stated that she would not betroth him, not in this lifetime.

He would carry a guiltstruck beast around on his shoulders until his dying day.

He'd invite self-destruction at every turn.

Voodoo Chile

The night the baby was born the moon turned a fire red. His poor mother cried, "Lord, the gypsy woman was right." Then she fell downright dead.

Little Miss Strange

Even on the other side, she was an anomaly. A ghost who held seances for her living son.

Long Hot Summer Night

His foster parents moved to Brazil when he was sixteen, hoping to save him from the legal traps that awaited his kind in the U.S. They sent him up in the hills and favelas of Salvador to find a white man of French origin who was once a scholar, but now seemed more interested in shamanism than academic honors. This white man's home was simple and almost cruelly spare. A dirt floor, a chair, a workbench, an incandescent bulb of no more than 40 watts that hung from a frayed cord over the picnic table at which he sat like a scrivener. A fossil of a man prepared to spend all of eternity documenting the 2,000 and some-odd plants used in Candomble rituals. For this he had abandoned Paris and the professorial life to live among the poor.

The boy (for that is all he felt himself to be as he cast a quick glance over to the man, furtively burrowed in his clerical task) was embarassed to even be in his presence. He crept out of the Frenchman's cabin as quietly as he had come. The sounds that suddenly rose up from his rustling shirt and leather-bound footfalls seemed to produce an oppressive, horrendous din.

Gypsy Eyes

There would be no marriage. The grandmother and the mother, though impressed with his manners, sensed he saw something in their daughter unwarranted and slightly unhealthy. They suspected that within him was a longing for her to become not the mother of his children but the mother he had never had.

Burning of the Midnight Lamp

Returning to the states meant returning to the quarantine camp reserved for his kind.

All the bloodbath-babies—all those conceived in the heat of the bloodbath ritual which had gathered so much force. Jumping from host to host like wildfire in the 'hood during the years and months his embryo was under construction in his mama's womb.

In the camp he had his own room, a sturdy, expanded porto-san affair with its own heating element, toilet, and wall-unit bed. He wrote himself love poems by the light of the heater, holding the thing aloft with one hand while his free hand scribbled sonnets to his own romantic virtues on the stall beside the shithole bowl.

Rainy Day, Dream Away

The long stay in the Amazon had made him crave sleeping under the stars during a rainshower while wrapped in a voluminous mango leaf. Night was also the time when the camp's exterior spaces were deserted. As devoid of human exchange as he generally preferred the world to be.

The rain was plentiful in Louisiana during the summer of his return to the states.

He got a lot of thinking done as he ambled nakedly across the grounds of the camp under cover of darkness. Everyone else, the rest of his quarantined and convicted brethren and sistren, shrank from the downpours. They all shivered inside at the thought of being caught dead in that deluge.

1983 . . . (A Merman I Should Turn to Be)

He wondered if he were turning into some kind of fish. He had not seen men who were half men and half fish while in Brazil but he had felt such creatures a possibility after going fishing with the deep-breathing specimens of African manhood who ventured deeper on lung power than he had believed humanly possible.

A summer of diving with them had increased his diving range also. In his own mind he set a fatalistic limit on how deep he could go before tempting the goddess of the crosscurrents, taunting her hungry undertow.

Here in the camp, though, he felt ready to expand his sense of aquatic boundaries.

With no bodies of water available, he became a mud diver, sucking his body as far down into the muck as the muck would allow, reversing the course to return to the surface bloodied, muddied, but unbowed.

After a few months of such activity, he reckoned, the next time I get down to sea, it could be forever.

Moon, Turn The Tides . . . Gently Gently Away

One day he got stuck in the mud. He stayed down too long. A flash rain had stopped as unexpectedly as it had started and the earth, the very topsoil in fact, began to bake and harden around his encased form. The crown of his head lacked the battering-ram force necessary to break the vaginal seal mother earth seemed set upon entombing him with.

A woman dug him out with her bare hands, extracted his traumatized figure from terra firma. Rescued him from the greedy matriarch who sought to bury whichever of her foolish sons returned his corporeal form to her for dispersal, dissemination, disintegration, and recycling.

The woman's name was Ashe but all her friends called her Aguaboogie on account of her love of dancing in the rain.

Still Raining, Still Dreaming

When the word came down that the camp and its inhabitants were being moved by boxcar to another state, he and Aguaboogie immediately began plotting their escape. All it required was another week of rain that would allow them to submerge undetected and finish building the cave that would sustain them until all searches for the escapees had been discontinued.

House Burning Down

They didn't so much hear the riot and resulting carnage from their lair as feel its sound and spiritual fury. While they had been planning a downward escape from the camp, other, more quotidian minds had been plotting an uprising. It was set to occur whenever the boxcars arrived. A last stand by all who carried the taint of whatever disease the State had concocted to imprison their kind.

He and Aguaboogie clasped hands in the darkness, daring not to stare in one another's direction. Each knowing the other was thinking the same awful thought: that the genocidal incineration of the camp would insure no one came looking for them among the pyres and the ashes of the massacred.

All Along The Watchtower

Her mourning for those above went on for what to him seemed an unnaturally long and unhealthy time. Finally he turned to her and offered a benediction: "You and I have been through this, but this is not our fate. So let's not talk falsely now. The hour's getting late."

(Two riders were approaching and the wind began to howl.)

Voodoo Chile (Slight Return)

Their Baby Child became a man who loved to treat grains of sand as if they were living things.

Sitting on the shore, greeting the sunrise, he was met by a gypsy woman—hair aflame, hands vigorously beating a tambourine. Making love to her was like being born again and again in a world without end, a world rising up and falling apart, forever imagining an eternity spent whirling about fragments of decimated matter and original sin, ordering them into form and being, capriciously, and at will.

Band of Gypsys, a film by Jimi Hendrix, with Yaphet Kotto, Foster Sylvers, Marpessa Dawn, Bill Gunn, Dick Anthony Williams, Richard Pryor, Gloria Foster, and introducing Jaco Pastorius.

The magnificent vista of Cambodia's Angkor Wat which opens this visceral film performs a tantalizing bit of misdirection. *Band of Gypsys* is anything but a genteel travelogue. Mr. Hendrix, having already distinguished himself as a novelist, short fiction writer, and illustrator of no small acclaim ("The Black Jack Kirby," claimed one addled admirer; "The Mocha Milton Glaser," gushed another) makes an assured directorial debut. His film is as up-to-the-minute as nightly news from Southeast Asia and as wrenching as Truffaut's *The 400 Blows.* Comparisons between the two films, in fact, could not be more apt.

Young Foster Sylvers, making his film debut as Noc, the orphaned son of a African American POW and a Vietcong prison surgeon, effectively melts the audience's hearts from the moment he appears on screen feeding from garbage cans in the streets of battle-torn Khe Sanh.

Though both parents are alive, the child, spirited away at the mother's request from Hanoi to a Saigon orphanage, lives among other mixed Black and Vietnamese boys. As they mature they come to form their own alienated but vicious street gang. Mr. Hendrix's handling of the boys' fast coming-of-age is full of refreshing candor and unsparing gristle. When Noc is set up by a prostitute for an assasination attempt by a rival gang, he barely escapes with his life, but loses his voicebox. He then invents a secret language of clicks, snaps, and hand rhythms by which his gang can comprehend not only his darkest intentions but his deepest feelings. Mr. Sylvers brings a winsome, almost wholesome appearance to Noc's brutalized innocence. He carries the weight of Noc's victimization in his eyes, but with little in the way of lachrymose sentiment. Befriended by Lewis Benton (played by Richard Pryor), a journalist on assignment from an Ohio chapter of the Black Panther Party, Noc returns to the U.S. with him.

Mr Hendrix's battle scenes display innovative camera techniques and emulsion treatments—the effect is akin to seeing war through a scrim behind which one senses more than sees cascades of blood and mounds of piled-up bodies. The audience experiences that heart-squeezing sensation of cardiac arrest that can set upon us in moments of true terror: that feeling that time is speeding up, slowing down, and standing still at the same time, that we are re-living our entire existence and that of the entire species in an instant, that we have never been more desperate to live or more assured that we have reached our end. We see it all through Noc's eyes, which are seen peering out from the frame's periphery in reaction to every single shot of an apocalyptic firefight.

When Noc and Benton return to Cleveland it is just days before the death of Martin Luther King and the paroxysm of violent retaliation which ensued. Defying his carekeepers' curfew orders, Noc ventures out into the streets to join the parades of looters ducking trigger-ready National Guardsmen on patrol.

How Mr. Hendrix got so much confident mobility from his cameramen is a mystery. How he restaged the Cleveland conflagration on a shoe-string budget is equally bewildering—the quick, centrifugal editing makes the destruction of lives and property seem far more violent than what is shown on the screen. Noc is unjustly convicted of participating in an urban disturbance and serves a year in a youth detention center before being deported. Upon returning to Vietnam he joins the North Vietnamese army, then defects in an attempt to find his father in the POW camp. In the nightmarish final third of the film, Noc is seen voyaging beyond Hanoi into Laos in search of his fabled parents.

The use of sound and music is by turns novel, chilling, and finally unsettling. Hendrix took pains to install a special play-back system in the theatre using multiple speakers. There is an effect of sound constantly swirling and panning around you, sometimes in anticipation of the action by nanoseconds. It's a film that relays and reveals more plot twists through sound than pictures, though it may take a couple of screenings before you realize just how brilliantly inlaid and hallucinogenic those aural cues are.

APPENDIX B

In which Stefanie Kelly Interprets What the Stars and the Planets Reveal about Jimi Hendrix

The day that he's born in Sagittarius is when the Sun is still making transit. Where he's born is called the Decadent, a period of ten days.

His day is called The Day of Electrifying Excitement and he is that entity. He moves on impulse, he's in constant motion, he's got a lot of nervous influence—like he was always moving, and there was never a period where he was still, not even off-stage. Not even when he was exhausted.

The other influence he has is The Hermit, a strong Virgo influence because of the numerology. The numerology is 27, which makes 9, and 9 is the card for Hermit. So that talks about him being a person who really needed to, more than I think he did, get time alone, like completely alone. Where he was looking within, where he was becoming more of who he really was or giving himself permission to be who he really is. He never got to that point. He died at the onset of his Saturn Return.

Saturn starts out at certain areas on the chart when you're born. So the day you're born you know as an entity what you're supposed to be doing with your life. But in talking, in learning to walk, talking to adults, getting punished, getting smacked down, you forget everything. And then as you make your transit to age 27 and a half, you enter Saturn Return boot camp training. Wherein Saturn, over the next three to five years, moves you to where you're supposed to be in your life. Now if you haven't decided to take responsibility for who you are, Saturn does often kill fire signs.

Turns out Hendrix was a double Sagittarius. So there was a whole risk going on, and he never had that moment of serious meditation without any drugs to interfere.

He had the strong Scorpio influence, which is a killer, and then he also had the Sag, which is a benevolent sign, but can be moved easily into all types of worlds. It, as well, talks about him having deep, long-lasting moods.

He needed both stability and freedom. That's why it was so hard for him to find a partner. He needed total freedom but he needed a mom, basically. His partner would have to be a mom. She would have to be someone who didn't mind supporting his every move and being there for him and didn't mind him fucking everybody and being gone for months at a clip. Or whatever.

What I think is interesting is the Yoruba deity Oya, goddess of the hurricane, comes up in this whole thing. Because you know when people die young they are said to have moved into Oya's house. And the reference that I used, which wasn't talking about any African gods, said he needed to control the inner hurricane.

His dark side was rash, rebellious, and frustrated. His light side was quick, intuitive. I don't get that he really had a strong dark side, to be honest.

His first house—the ascendant, the face that you show the world—that was Sag. So he was all that, all the freedom, all the movement, that was really him, he wasn't acting. That's how he really felt.

Now how he felt about all of that past-life/mom stuff would be talking about his moon, and his moon sign was Cancer. I haven't really looked into it that deeply yet, but I'm going to assume from the moon in Cancer that he had serious mom issues. He might have thought she was crazy at some point. The mom might have been a little bit crazy at some point. But she also formed his personality and so much of his life seemed to depend on what she felt about him. I don't know if she was alive or dead. So there's the mom, the past-life, the stability, the security, he really wanted those things. But there was no way for him to get those things. He definitely needed women around him but he didn't need those women to overpower him.

At the onset of your Saturn Return you choose really difficult relationships, and I believe the woman he was with when he died was a Scorpio. It was the wrong kind of energy for him. It was jealous, it was binding, controlling, too much.

What he wanted was that emotional, watery thing that the Cancer moon gave him, and he saw that similiarity, but the difference between Cancer and Scorpio is Cancer is cardinal water, the essence of the element. Scorpio is *ice* of water, a whole other situation. They're not the same. He thought it was the same and was in so much emotional pain, he was distracted.

His Venus was in Sag and he really would have done well with another Sag. Strangely, because double relationships don't always work out, but he would have done well. That or an Aries woman who's fucking as many people as he is, and really doesn't care.

If I could have introduced him to a Chaka Khan at that point, they'd probably still be together.

His second house, house of possessions, was ruled by Aquarius, and Aquarius doesn't really care about possessions, so he didn't seem to have a lot of possessions. That wasn't his thing.

The third house, the house of siblings and also house of communications, was in Pisces, and totally murky. He wasn't understanding his family or his siblings if he had any at that point. Pisces either swim to the bottom or the top, and he was at the height of communication in his art, but in his life, it just shut down on him.

Fourth house, house of stability, ruled by Aries, which is hilarious. With Aries ruling your fourth house you're talking about always feeling like you're making a home, always beginning with the home thing. It's always a new start. You find things are beautiful but am I going to get any stability here?

Now, fifth house, house of creativity—his creativity was the most stable thing about him. Obviously it's what got him money, what set him up for the rest of his life, set people around him up. He never had any confusion about that.

The sixth house, health, and the seventh house, marriage, I'm going to link those up. I've not only got those ruled by Gemini, which is a lot, but the sixth house of health and service has also got Saturn in it. That's a lot. Saturn begging him, and then *making him* take responsibility for his choices around how he treats his body. There's duality in that house as well. There's some things he may have thought about, like being a vegetarian, but he never thought about not doing speed.

The house of marriage, the seventh house, also talks about feelings of duality. Cancer is another sign, like Gemini, that appears to want one thing, but actually wants another. So now he's got the double confusion of Gemini ruling that house and feeling two totally different ways about relationships. He felt none of us should ever have a situation where we're bound to one partner—the double Sag working with the Venus ruled by Gemini would say that. Be like, Why should I not explore who I am, completely, and in different relationships at the same time? That was who he was.

During that era there were a lot of men who used that as game and he really wasn't using that as game. He really believed that. And he could handle that. If she's fucking too, well, then let's get together later and talk about it. He was on a real freedom thing.

Eighth house, of sex, death, and taxes, is in Leo, a sign that is quite expansive and arrogant. So there were certain dues he really didn't believe he had to pay. If he never paid taxes, that makes sense to me.

In the ninth house, house of travel and learning, he was ruled by Virgo, and interestingly enough, he didn't love traveling as much as we think he did. It was who he was but he wanted to stay home, or create a home, have someone there who understood him and have a stable base to go back to.

Ninth house also shows he had a lot of humility and was constantly being about perfection of his art. Virgo is funny—we will allow someone a lot less talented but more confident to get on before we do because we never want to present anything to the world that's less than perfect. He took over the spotlight because of who he was but he would push other people to the forefront. He would not present himself before anybody else. He had a lot of humility in those kind of situations. There were people who wanted to work with him and he was very humble and very analytical. In terms of his art he was his own best critic. He was great at it in fact.

He really was a very sweet, easygoing guy in so many ways. He just let the people around him completely fuck him. Cancer is a dangerous moon, because it's ruled by the moon, a shadowy, fluid presence and it is a pain in the ass to have your emotions go though that many changes every two and a half days.

Cancer moon also brings delusions. *In a normal state.* You don't have to be high or anything. So if you add drugs to that mix, or vipers in your circle, you got a lot going on. He was literally seeing things. And he wasn't crazy.

The tenth house was in Libra, so he wanted riches but he wanted his riches to be in balance with the rest of the world. He didn't see any reason for him to have money while somebody else was starving. He was really that humanitarian dude.

Eleventh house, house of friends and associates, ruled by Scorpio, so there you go. You've got that heavy controlling influence from friends. So there were a lot of times when he had to cut off relationships, dead them, because he had to be like, What the hell is going on?

Twelfth house, house of hidden enemies, ruled by Sagittarius. So in a lot of ways he was his own worst enemy, because of past issues of insecurity. There'd be situations where he could have taken one path but he took an easier one, there was that level of self-destruction.

Mercury in Sag—he loved to talk. Never thought he was making his point, but he loved to talk.

Venus in Sag. That free-thinking, loving being who liked to take care of his women.

Now it seems he had a very bad temper—Mars in Scorpio. The stories about him hitting women are a deep possibility. Women not talking about it I can also see because he was so sweet that they didn't want to even remember, like it didn't happen.

He was a natural pimp because he could have had three wives and it wouldn't have been a thing for him. Then there's that fire sign that is always reminding me of Shango because they're talented and beautiful, and light up a room, but they also have the potential to beat up on women, and be pimps and be users. They grow out of that, and he's philosophical enough that he would have realized, This is wrong, and he would have stopped. But he didn't have a chance—he was a baby when he died.

Jupiter in Cancer—Cancer's one of the luckier signs in the zodiac and Jupiter is about expansiveness. Jupiter understands the moon in that the moon wants things to go a certain way, wants things to be based on intuition. Jupiter has a fiery intuition and talks about good luck and bad luck, and when his was good it was great, and when it was bad it was terrible. So his luck was great, but not because he hadn't really tapped into his intuition.

Saturn in Gemini means he could have taken total responsibility for everything or taken none at all, or found a balance between the two. What he liked to do was shift between the two, because when you do that, no one gives you an excuse to do the other.

Uranus, planet of invention, a choice between whether he wanted to take the light side or the dark side of invention. If he was going into his Saturn Return his invention was about to go into a darker side than ever before, because Saturn's color is black and it's heavy, and it's about limitations and responsibility. And you feel crazy, especially if you're that person who's been running around the world not giving a fuck. So we would have seen some really *out there* looks from him, some serious duality shit.

I'm reminded of David Bowie when he became Ziggy Stardust and adopted alter-egos. Hendrix would have adopted alter-egos. He would have had three alter-egos. Like there's Jimi, Ja-mae, and Hendrix, and you'd know who each one was because they'd all have pretty distinct personalities.